Cort's Royal Ink
Tattoo Company
Presents

Cherry Blossom Coloring Book

All Artwork and layout by
Cort Bengtson

ISBN# -13: 978-1-948187-30-5

Please respect the Art and ,
replicate don't duplicate.
Thanks

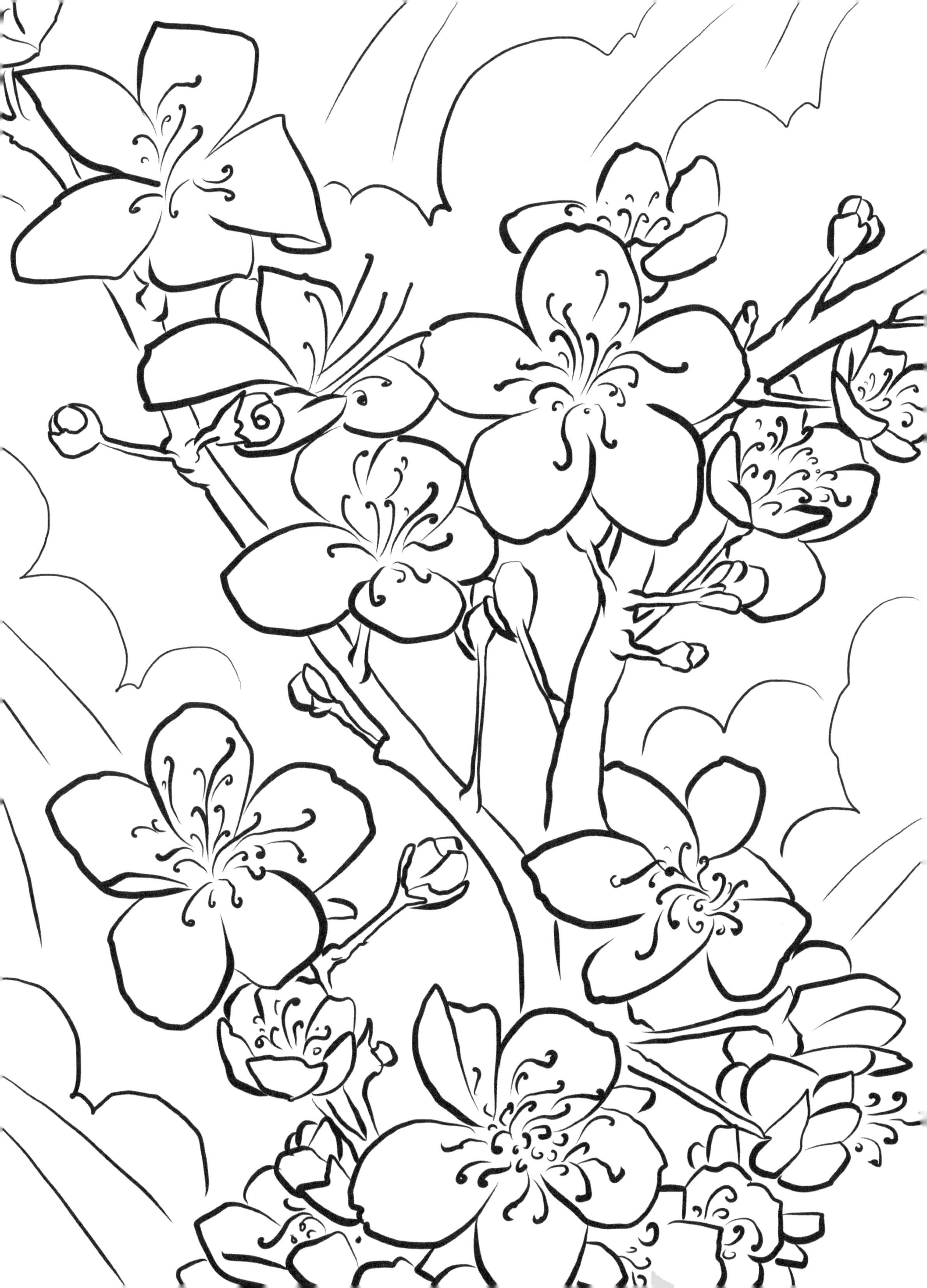

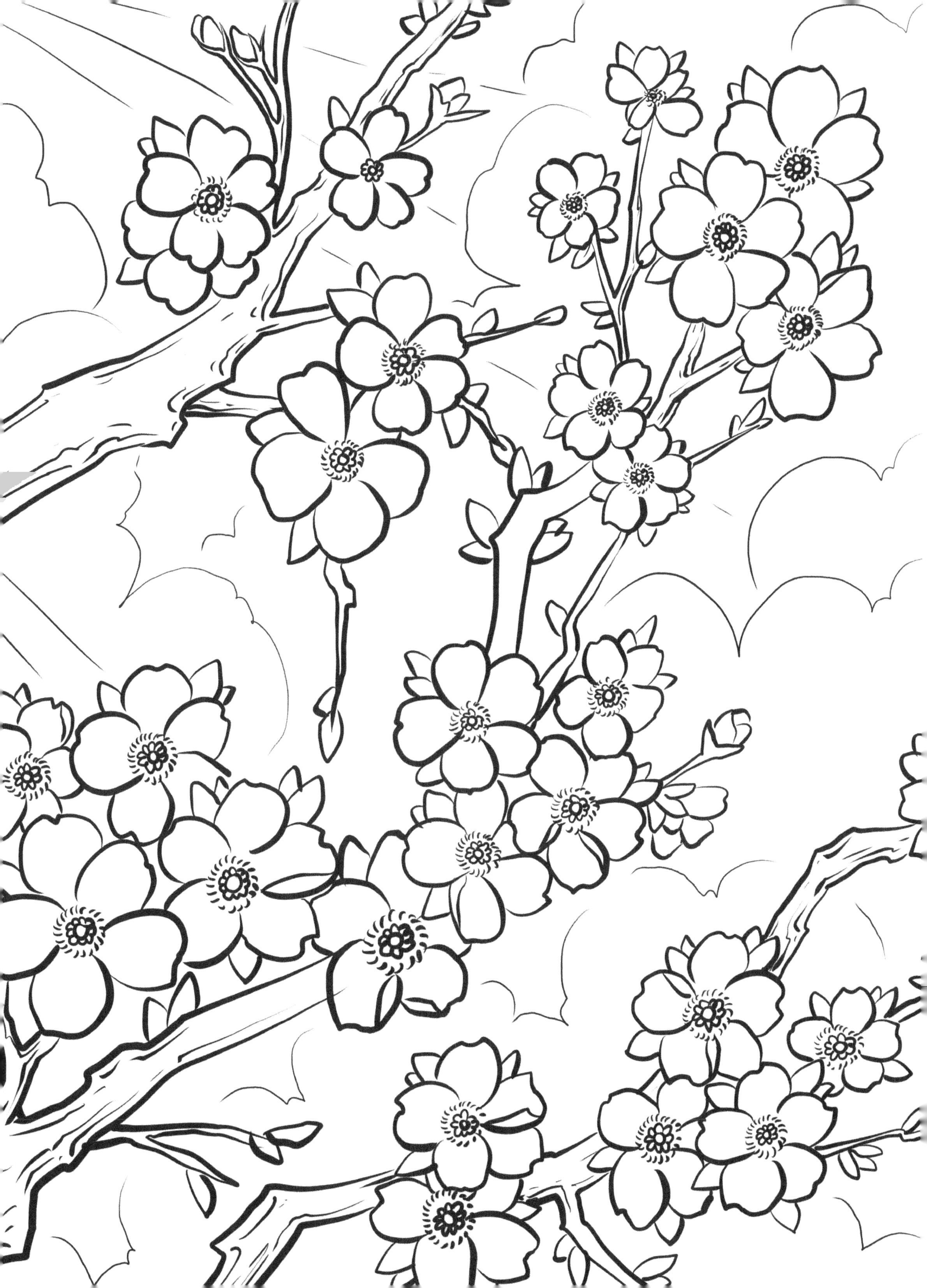

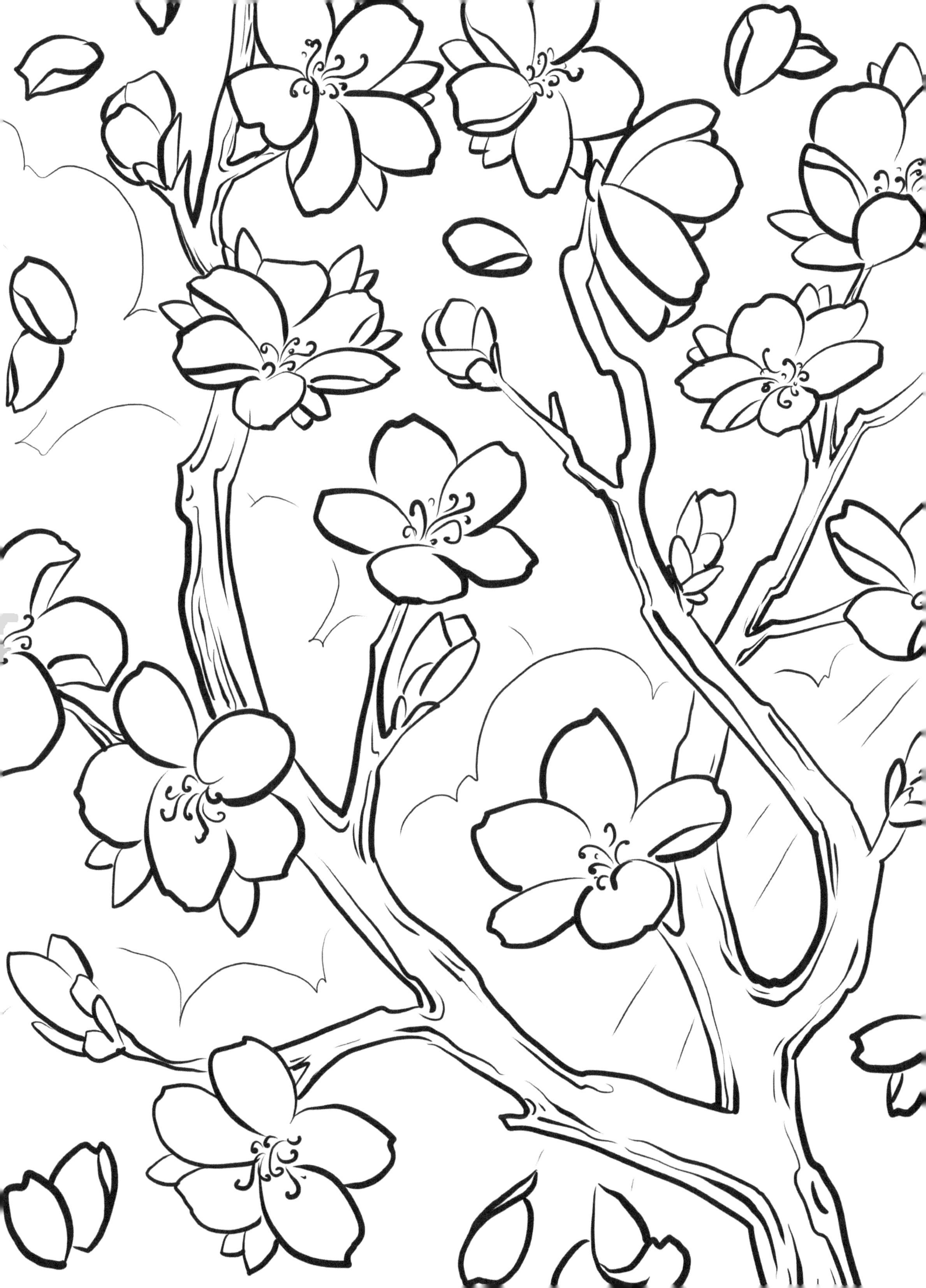

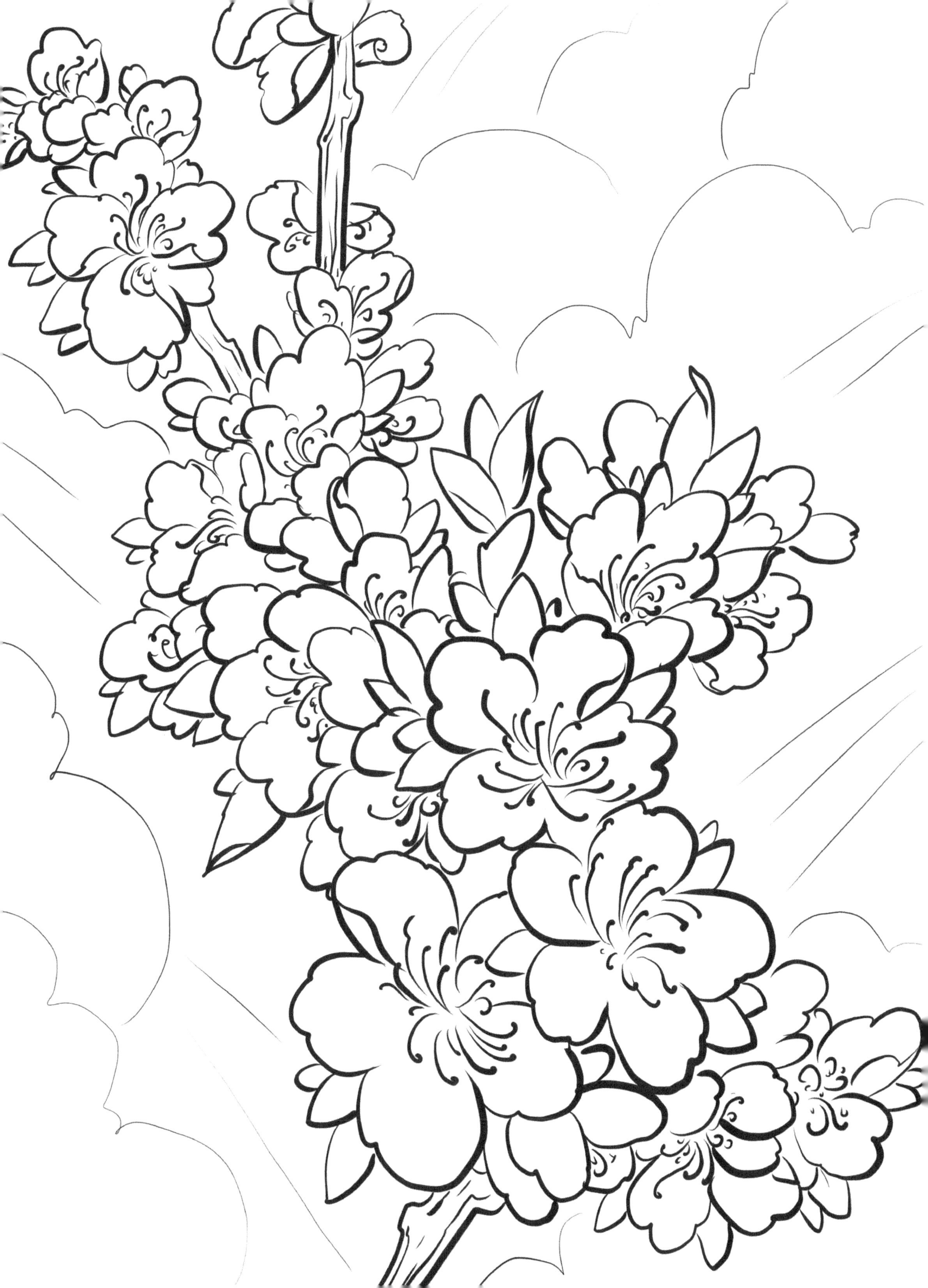

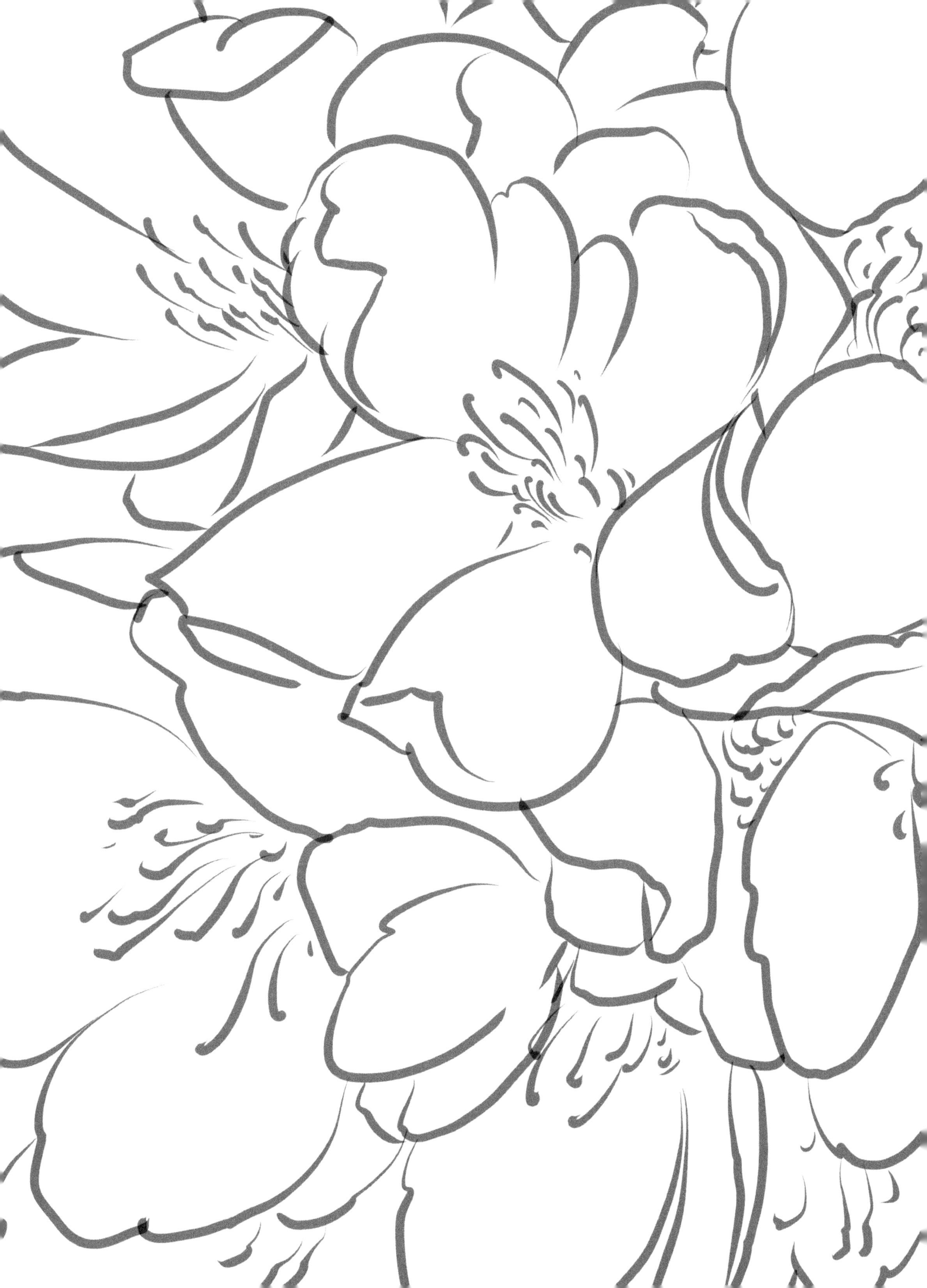

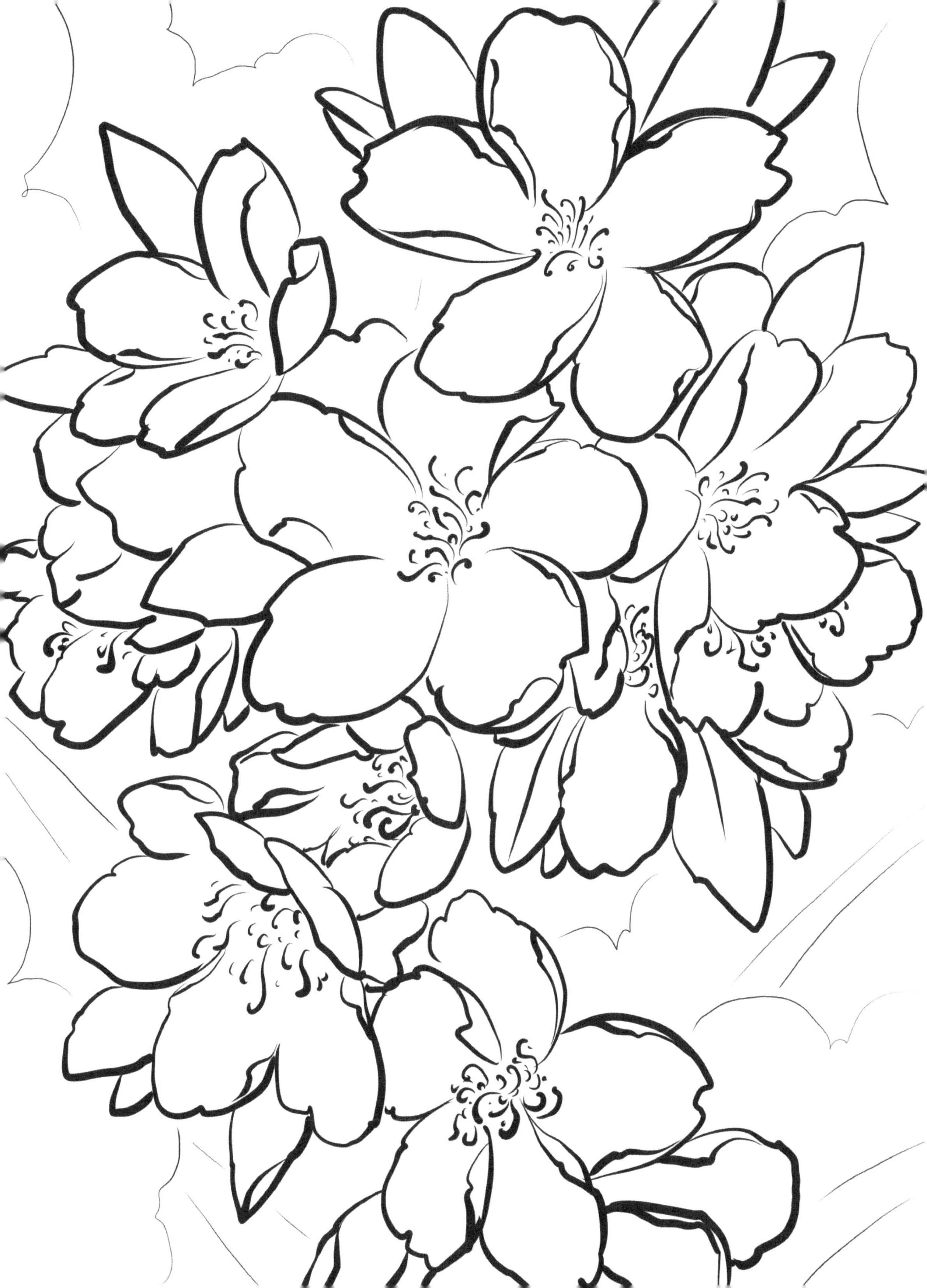

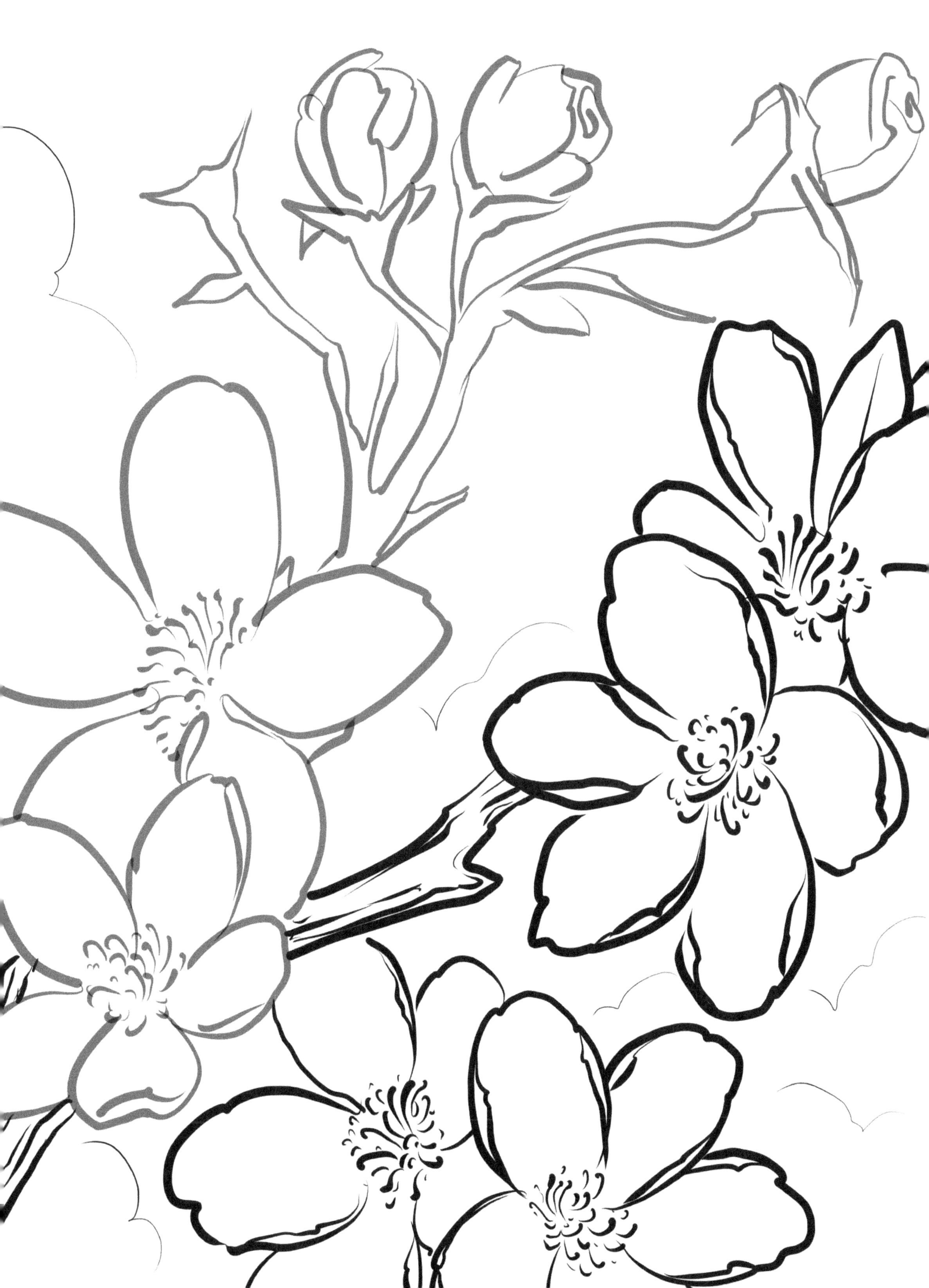

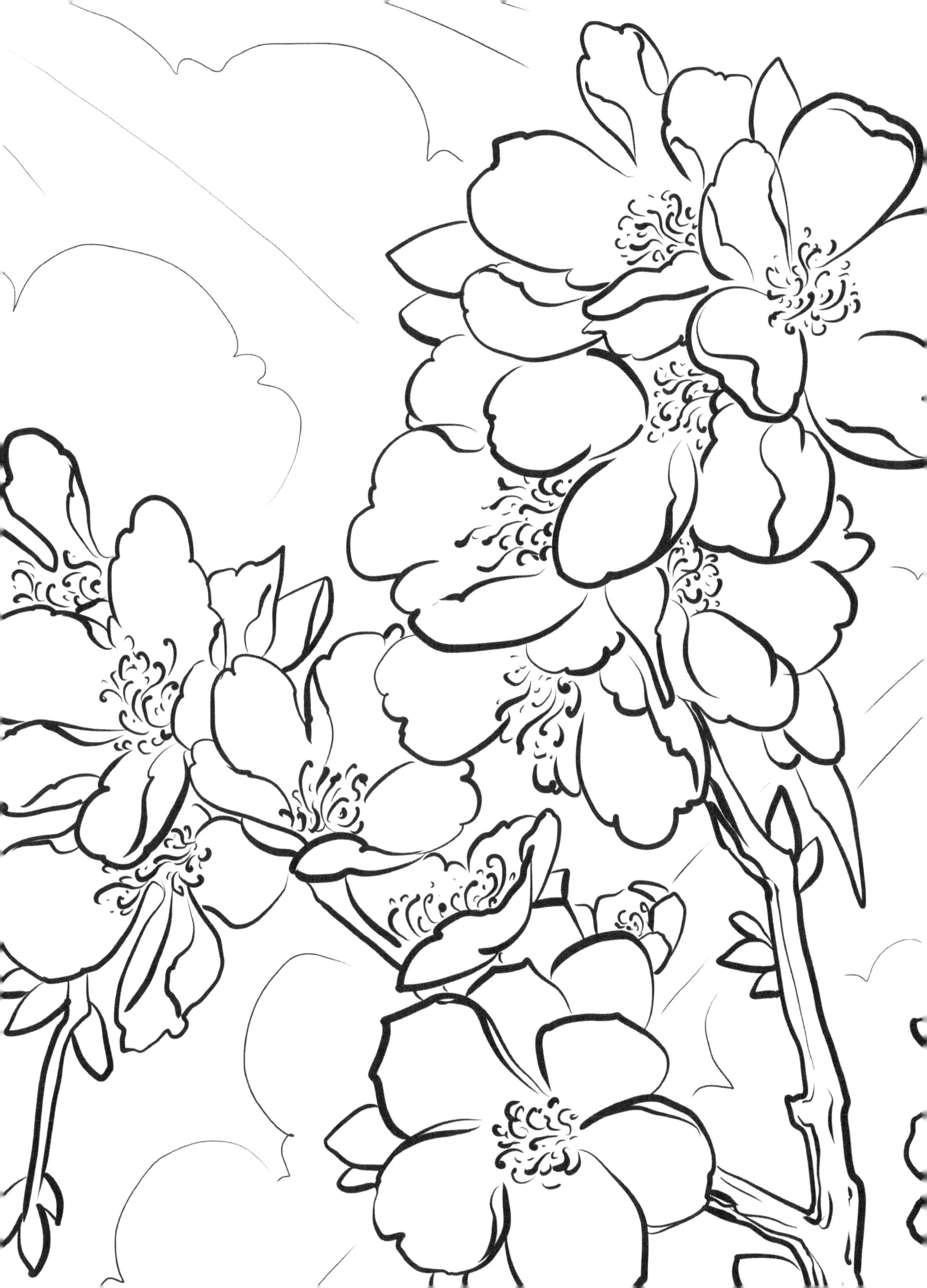

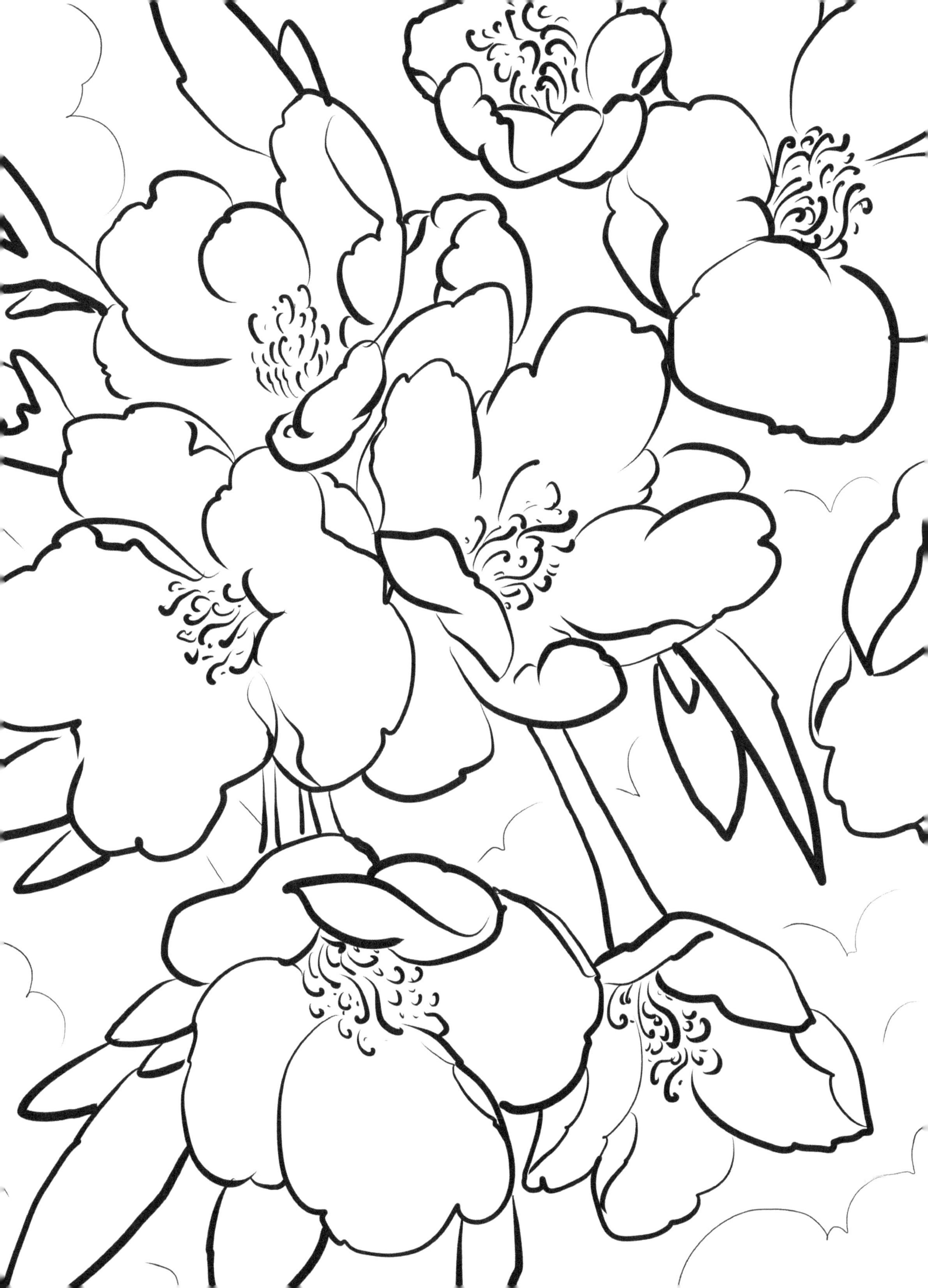

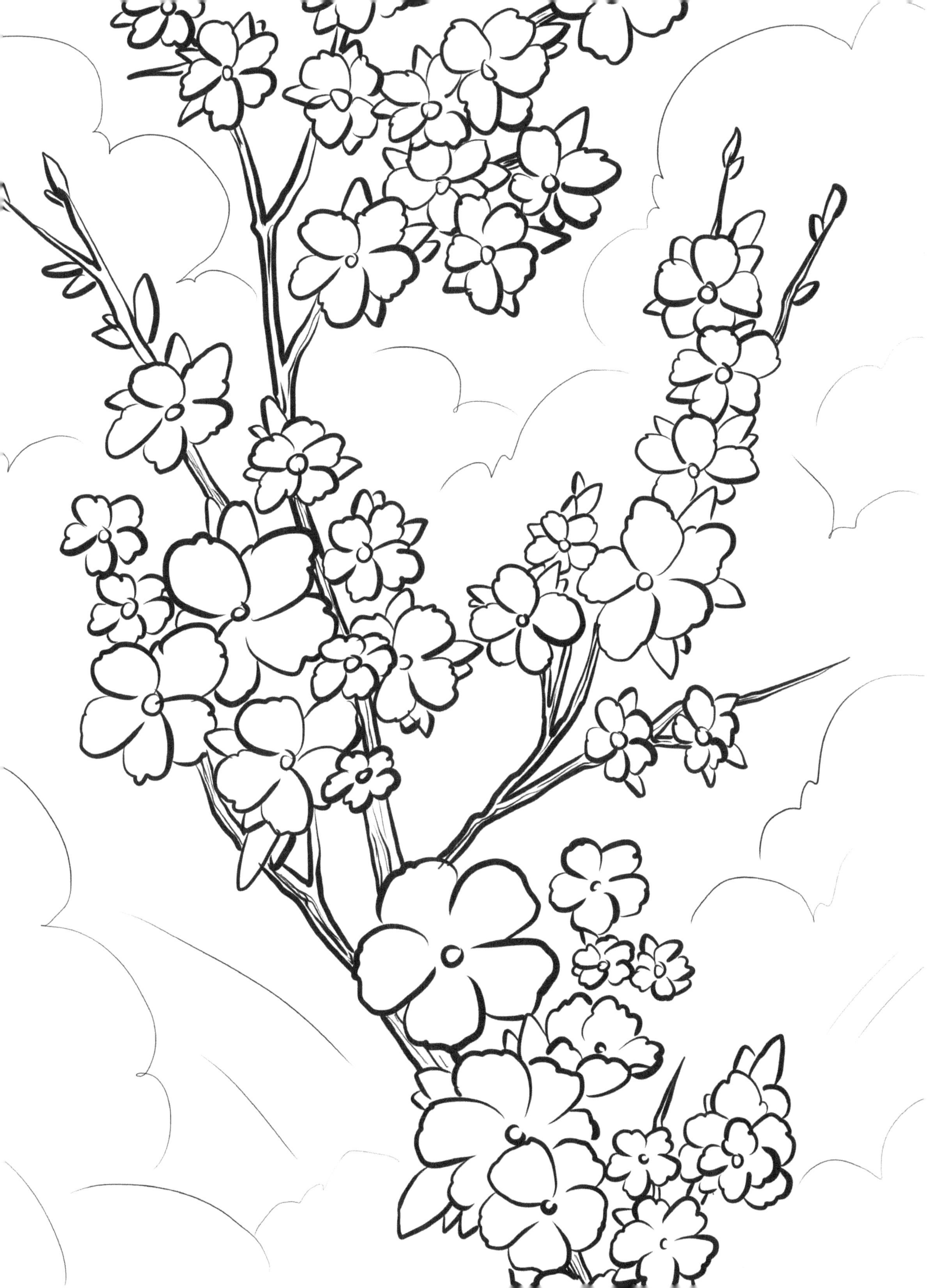

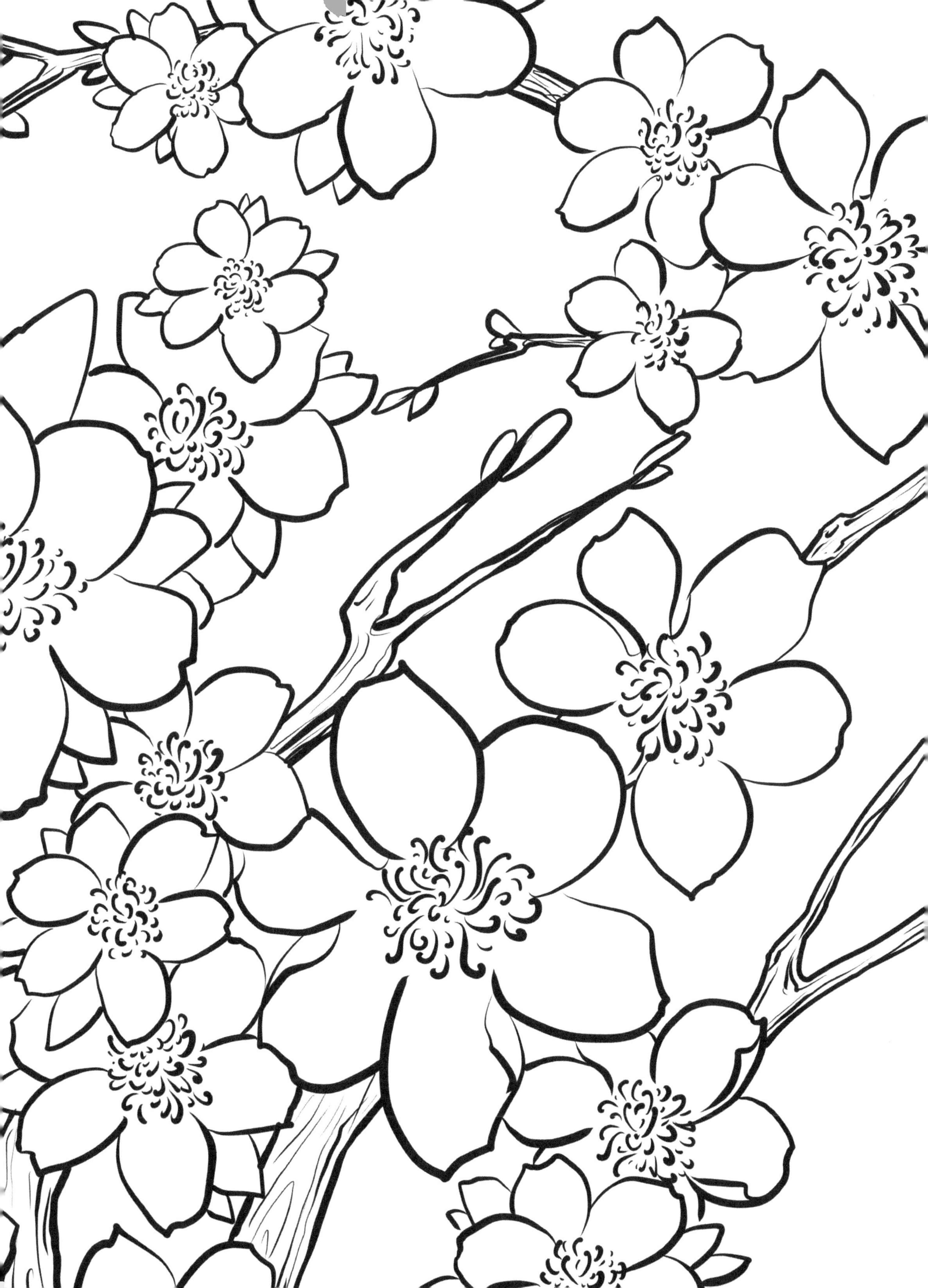

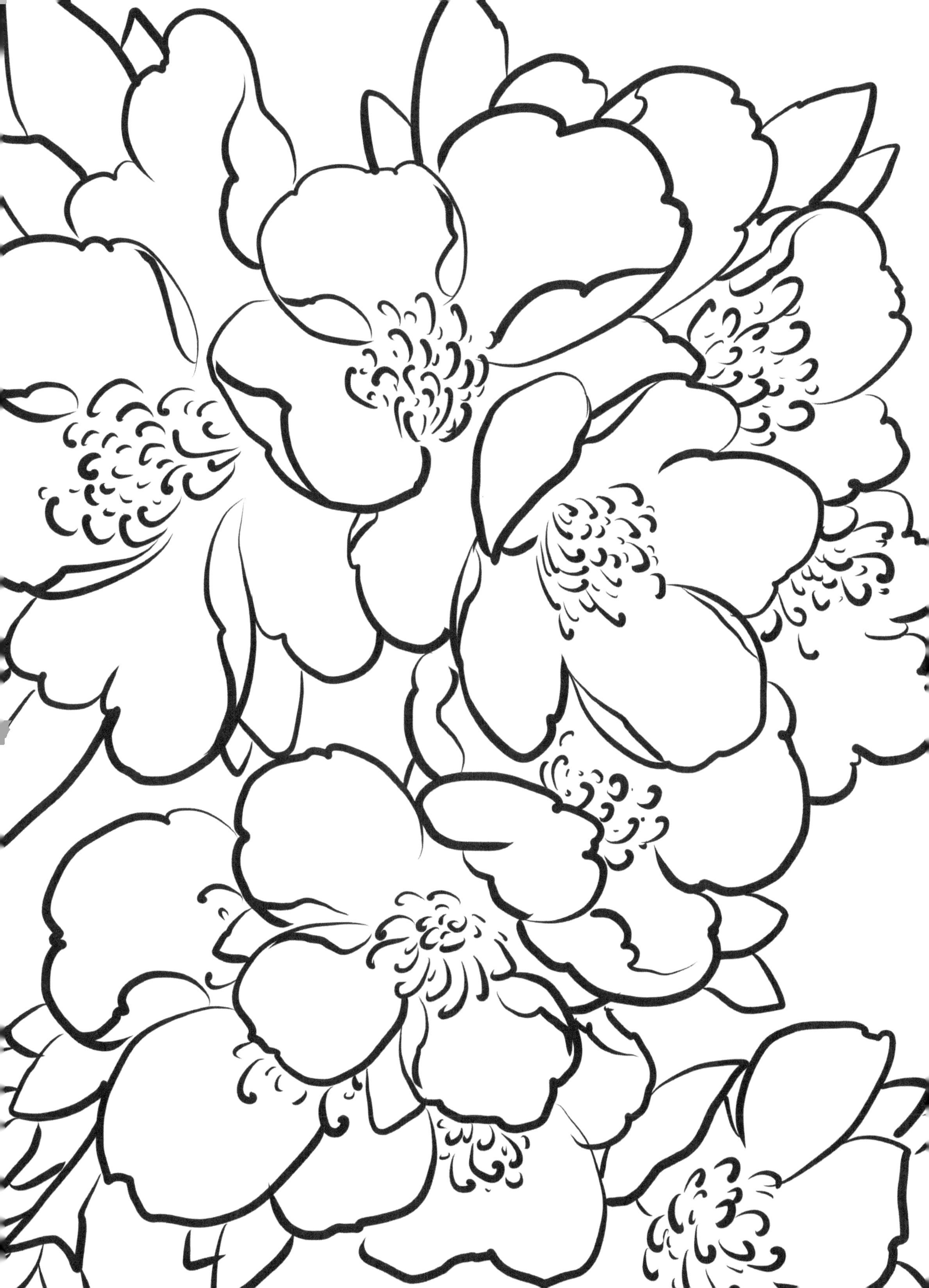

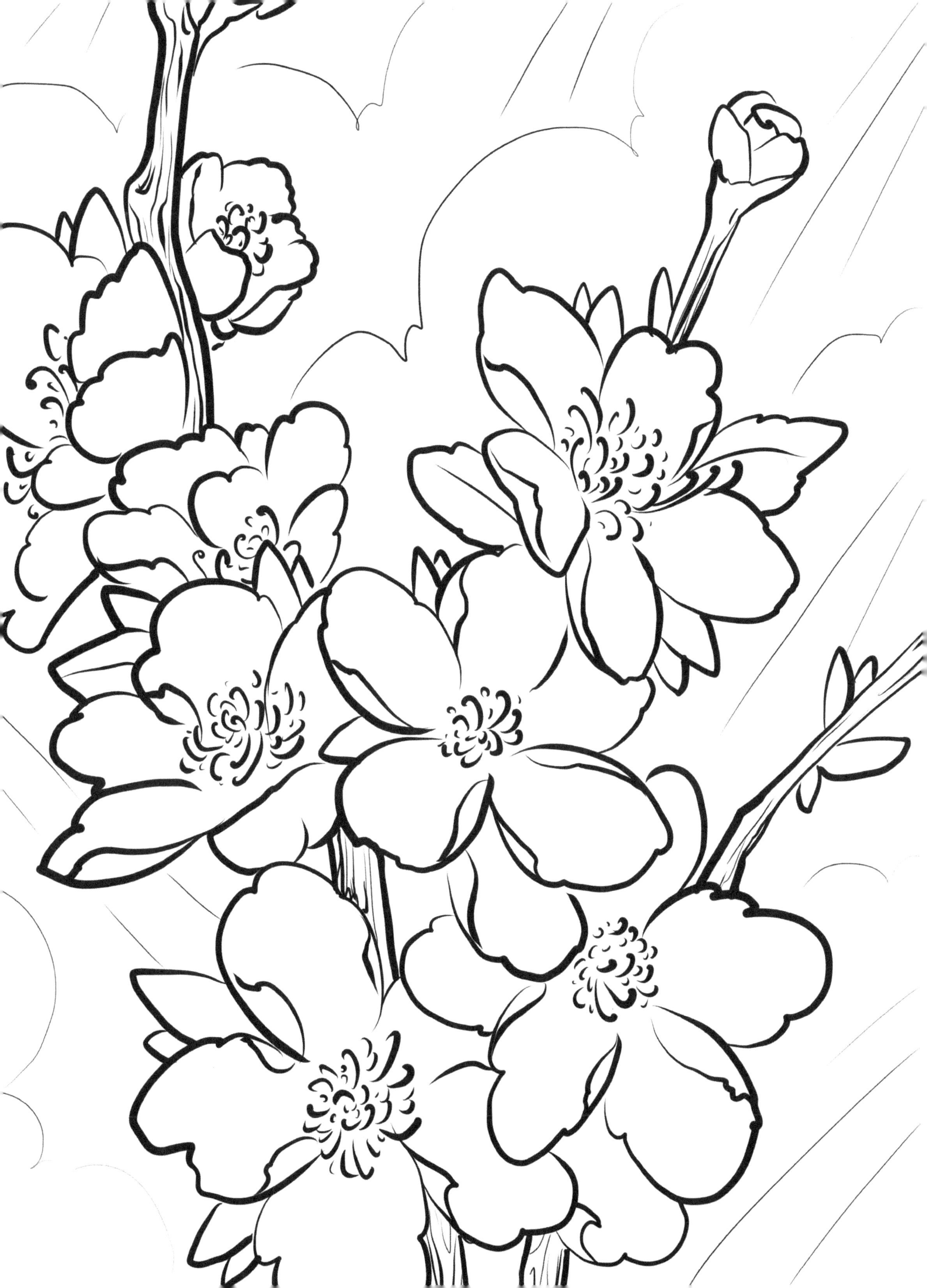

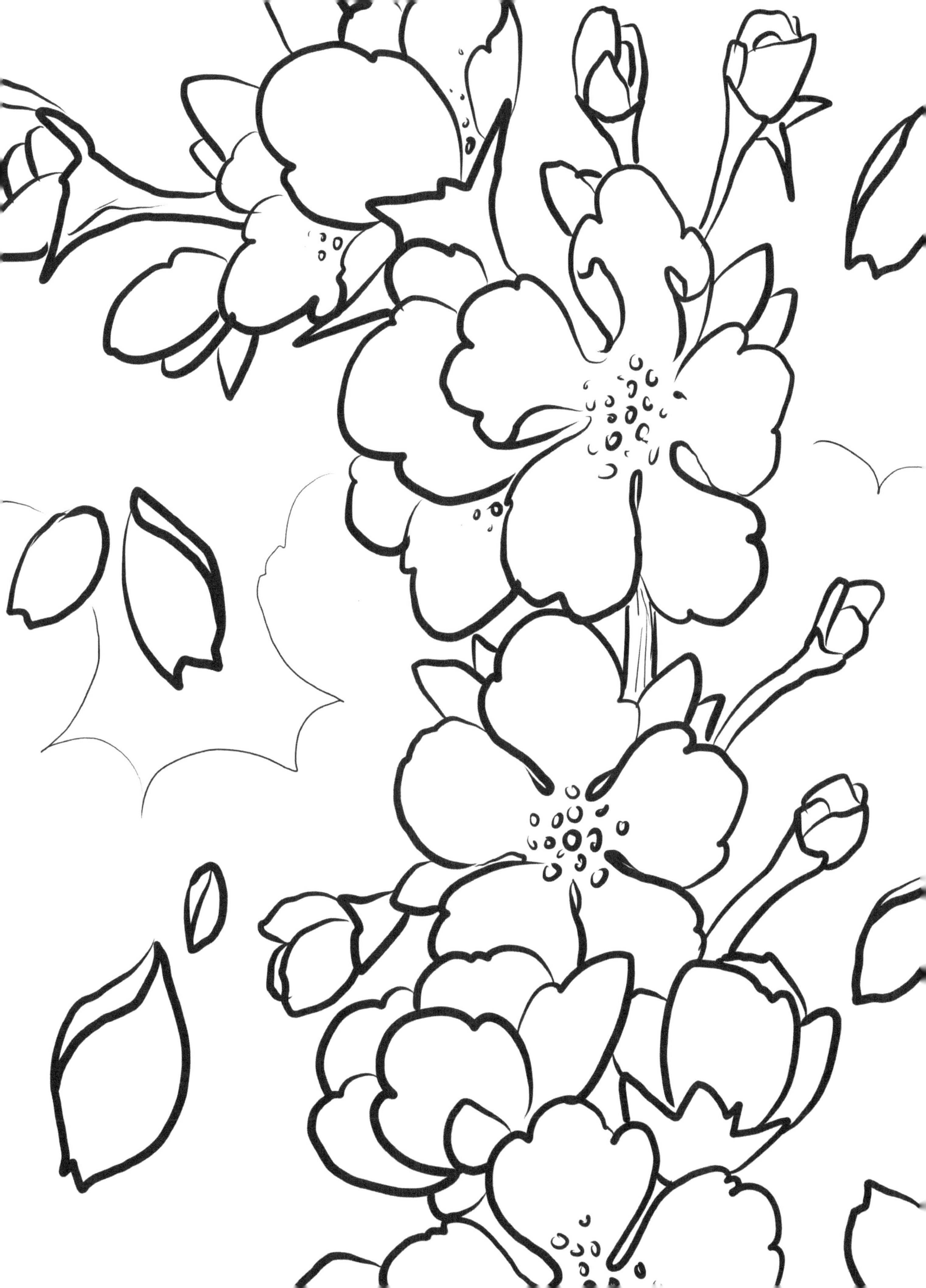

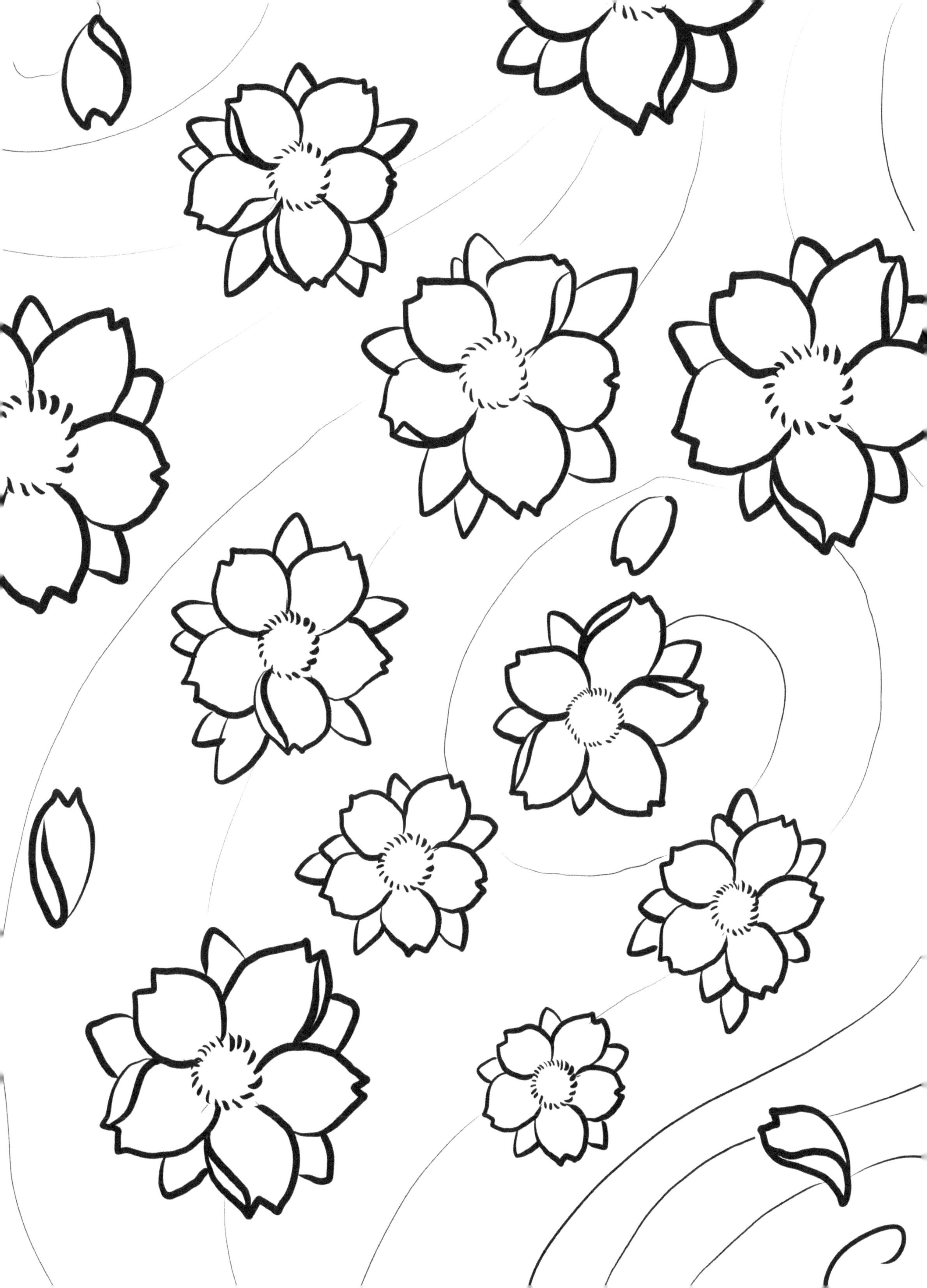

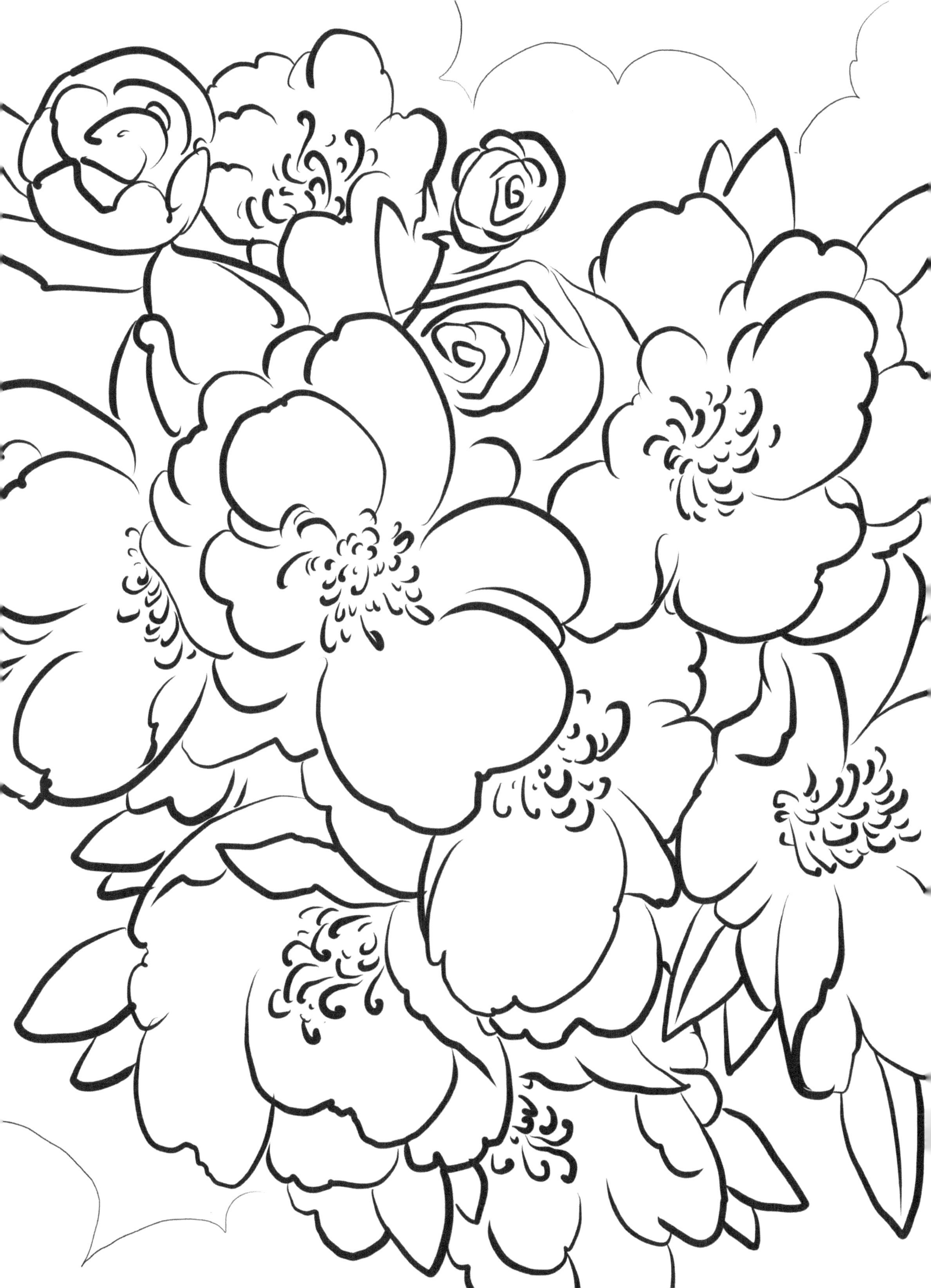

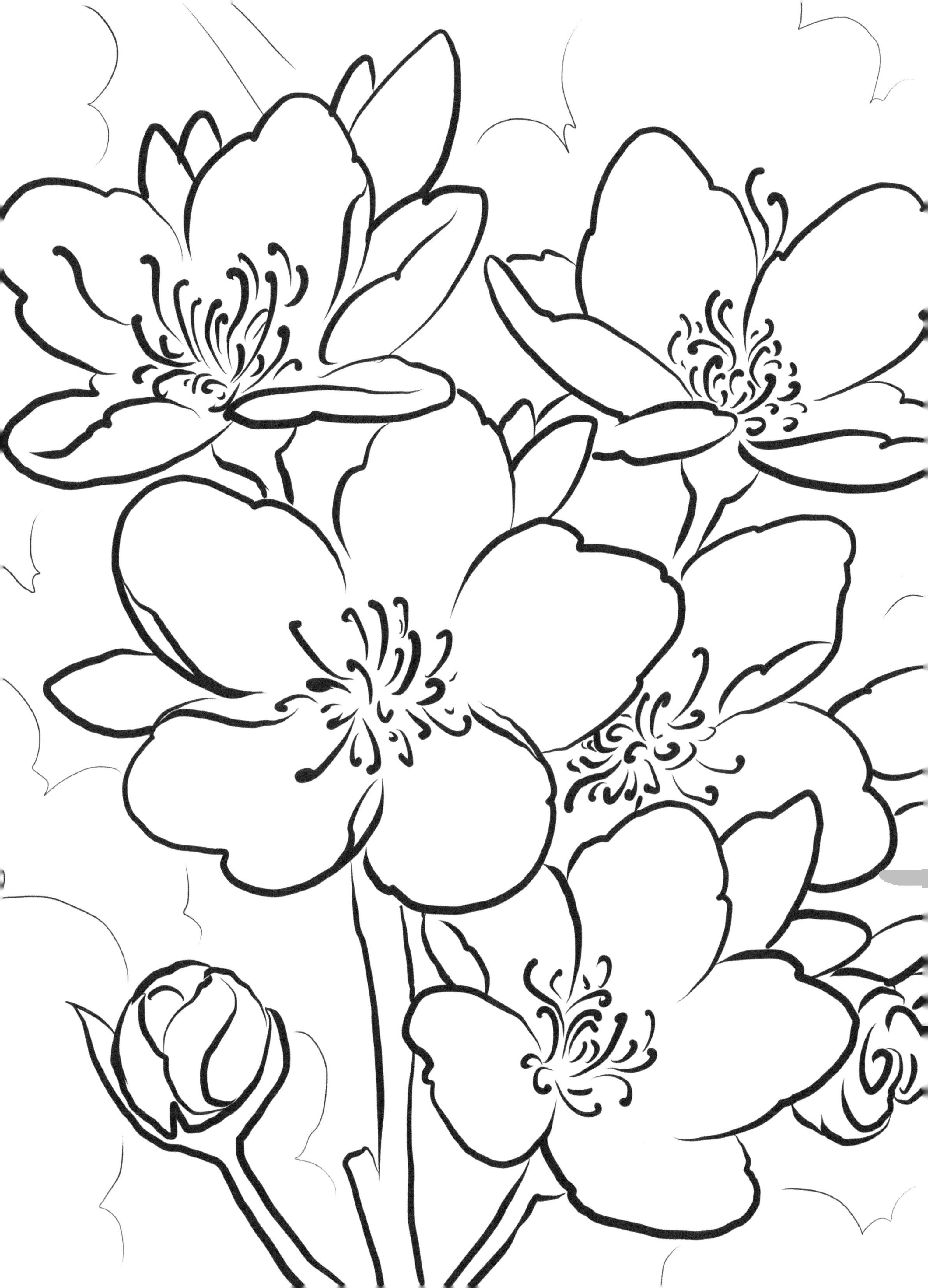

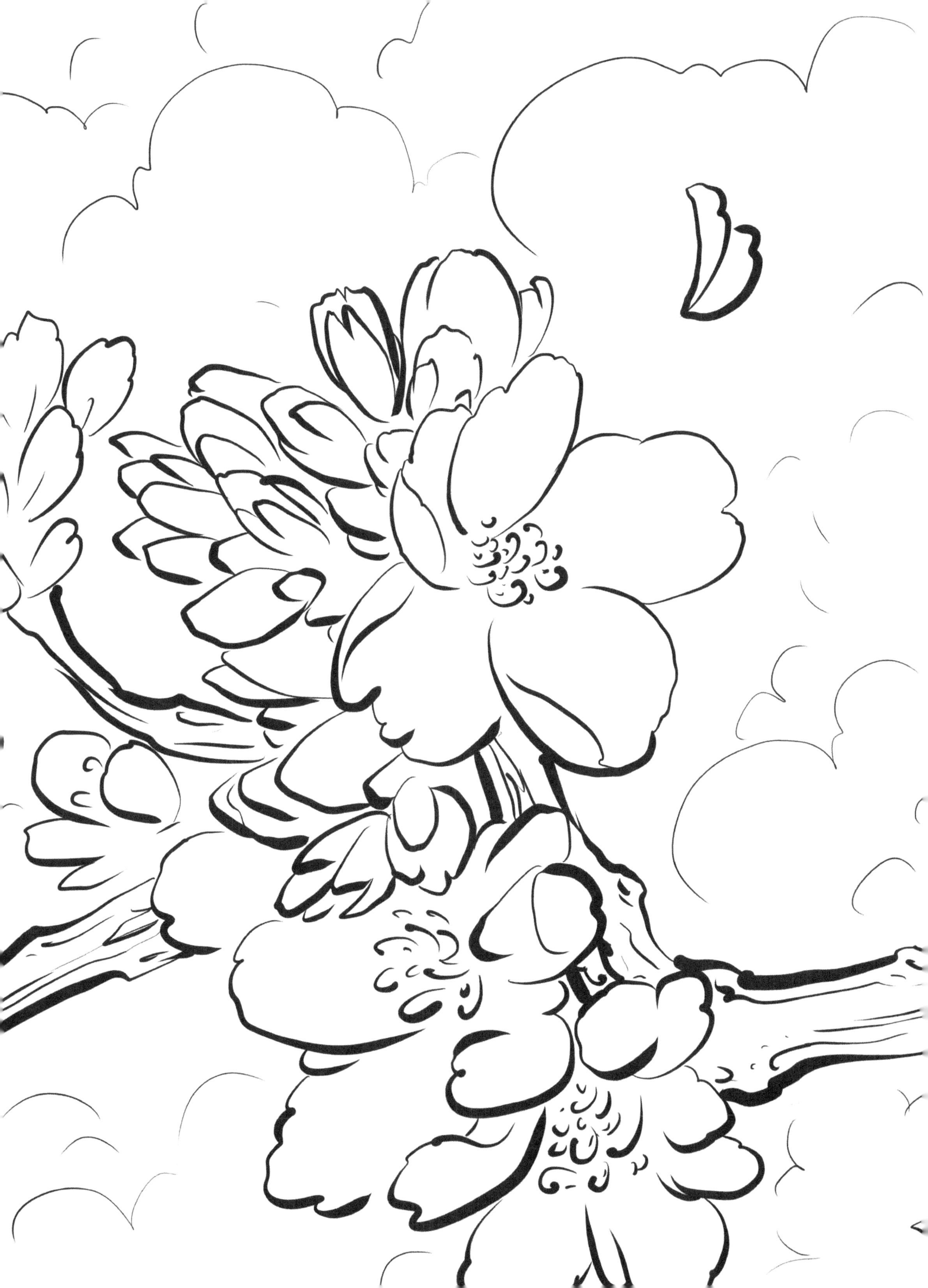

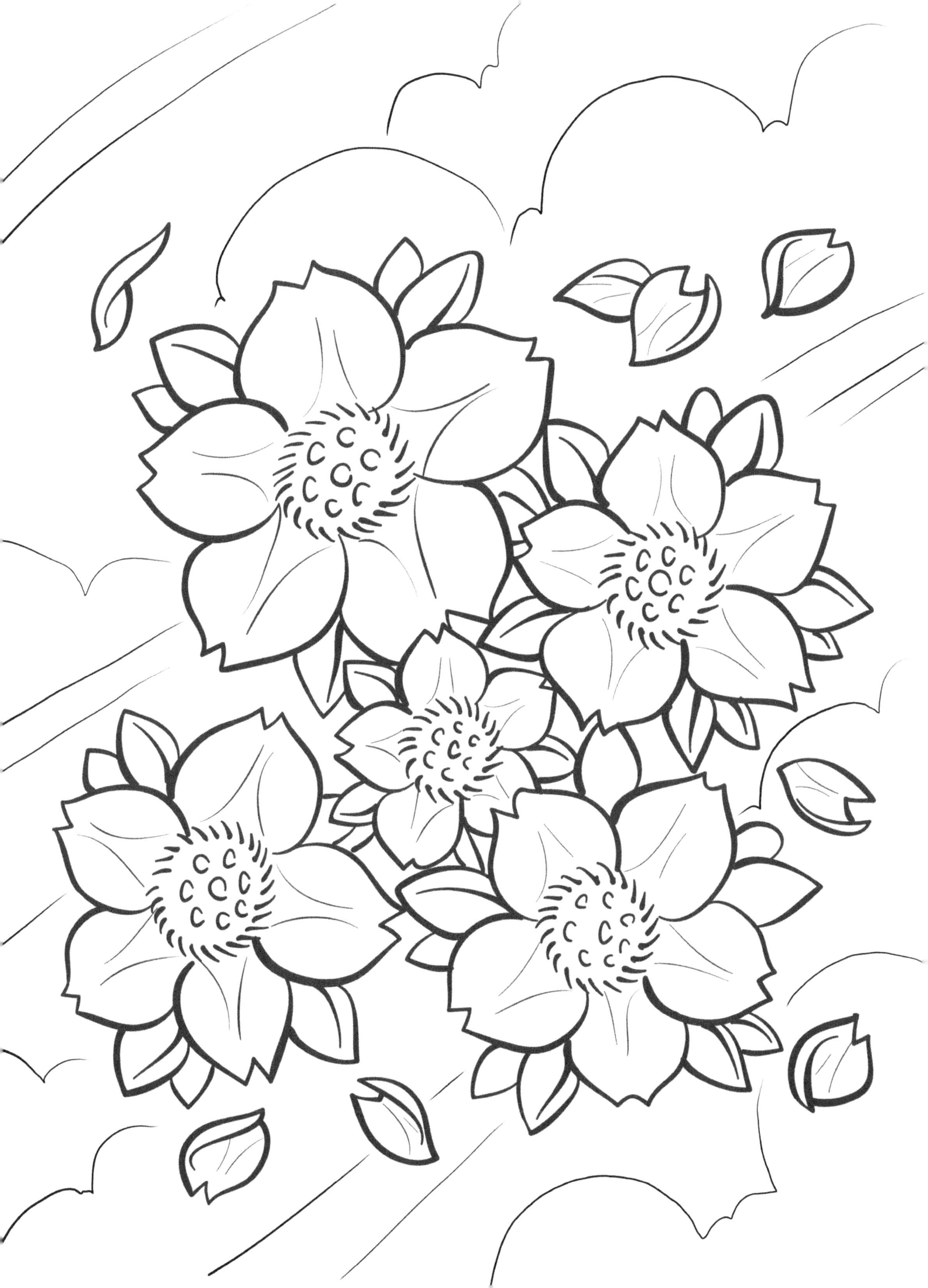

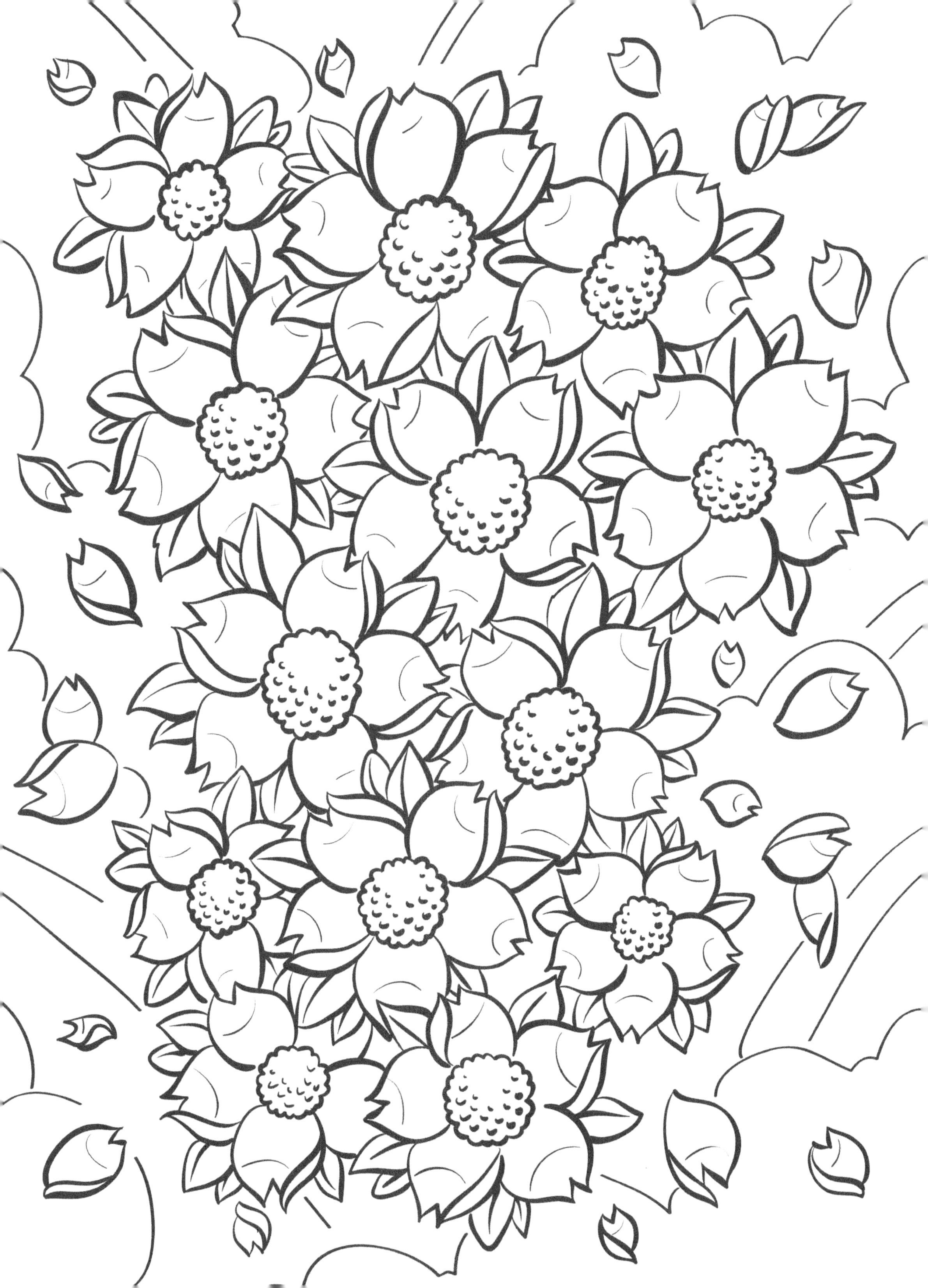

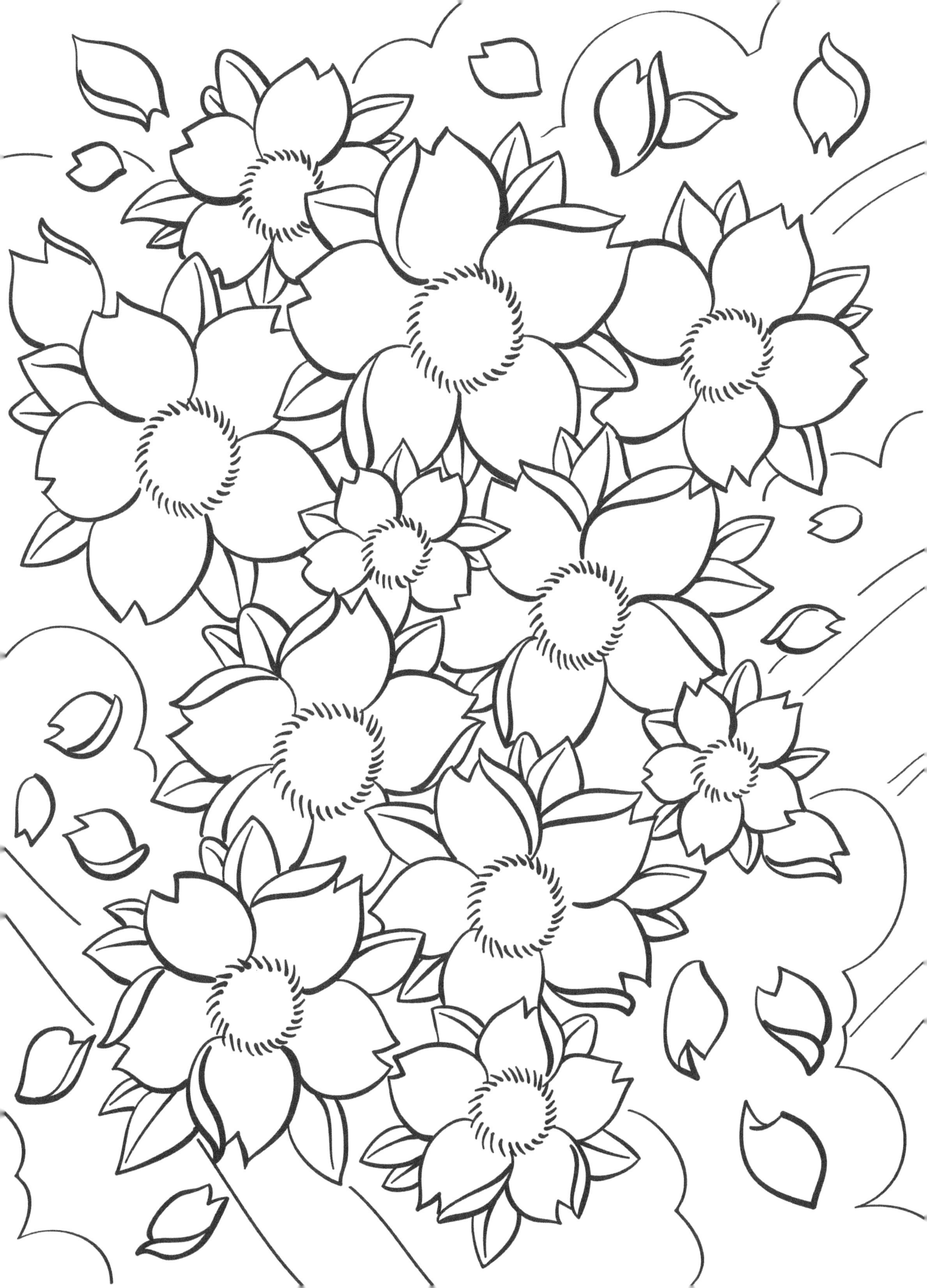

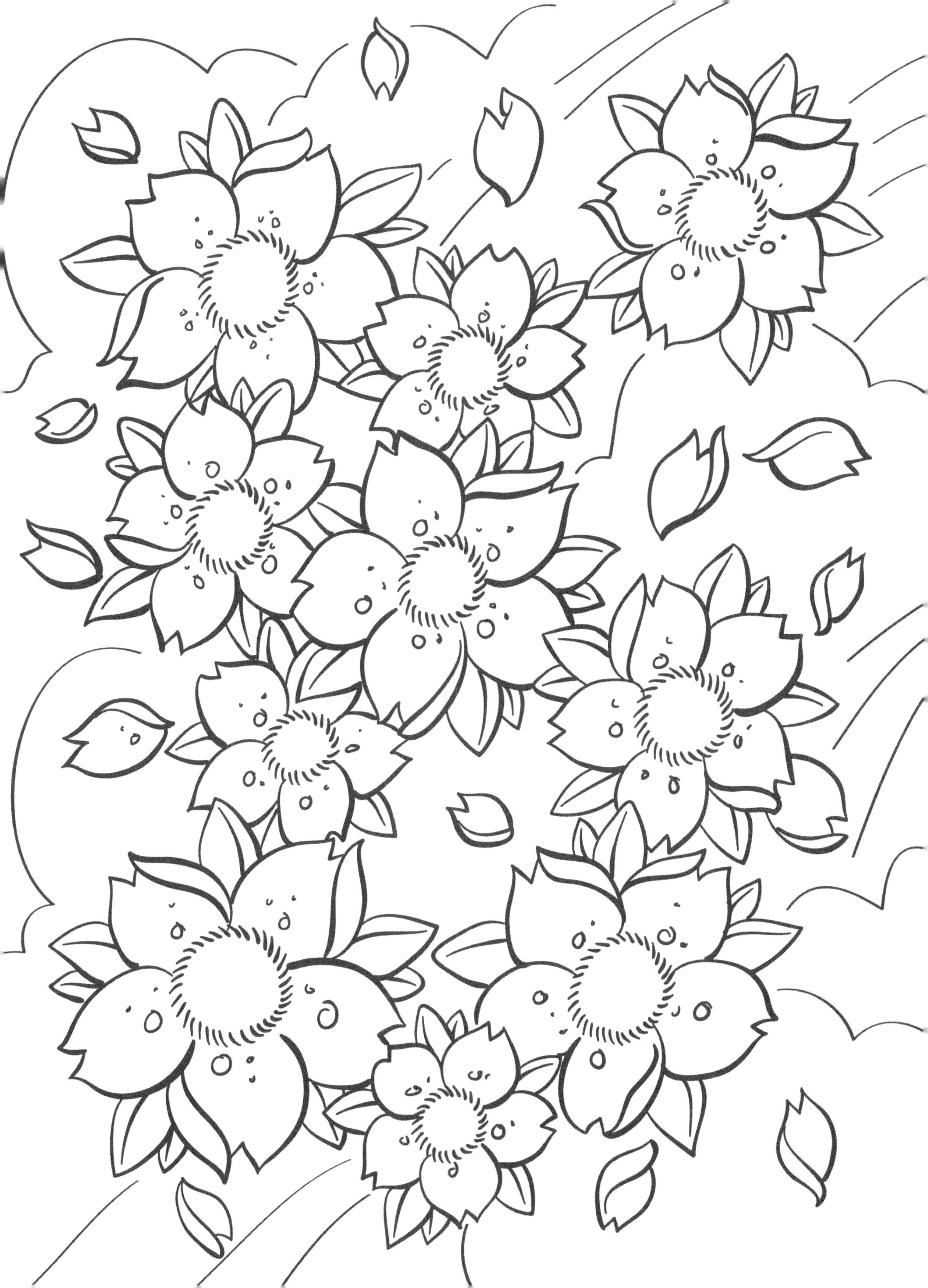

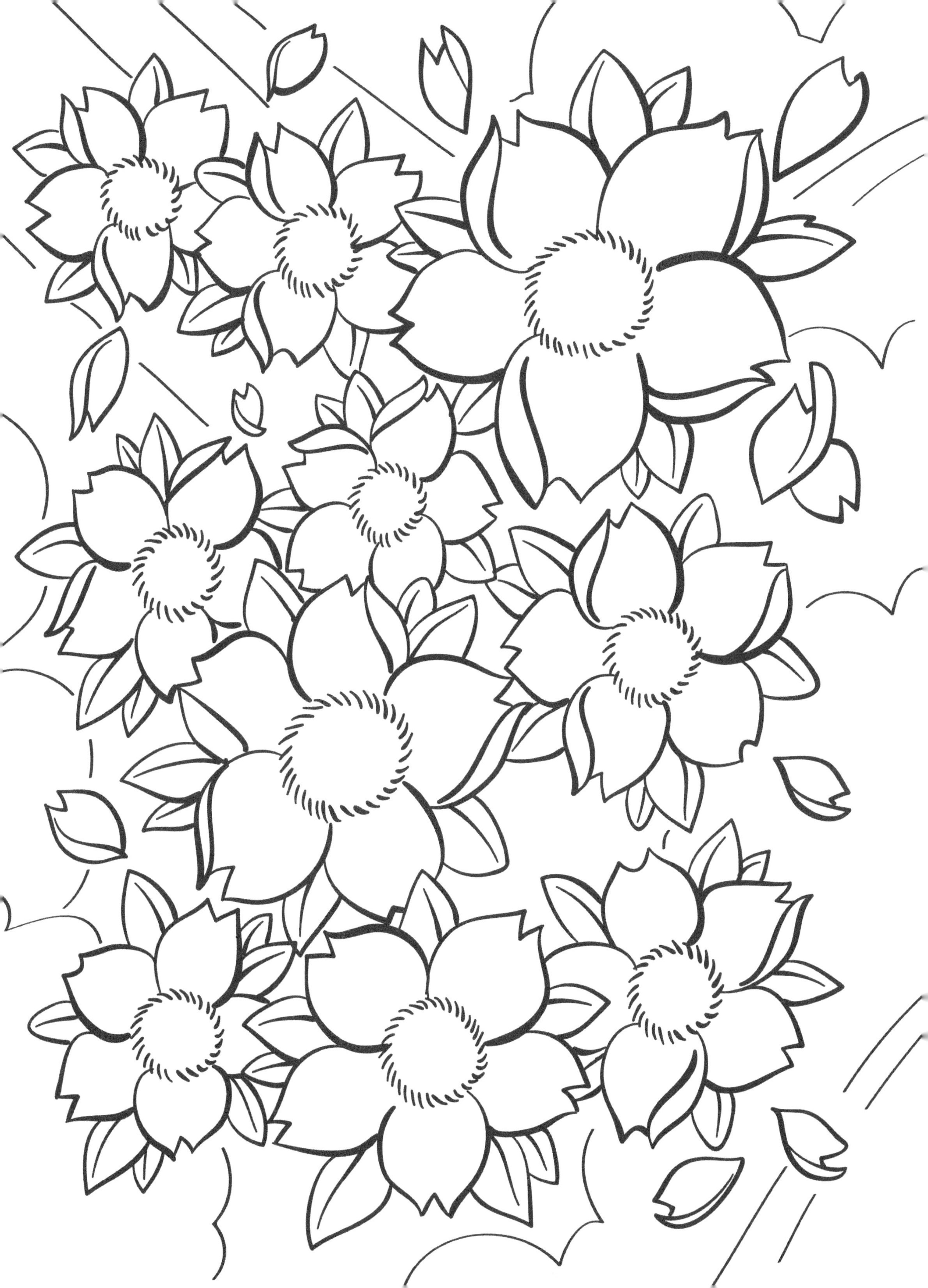

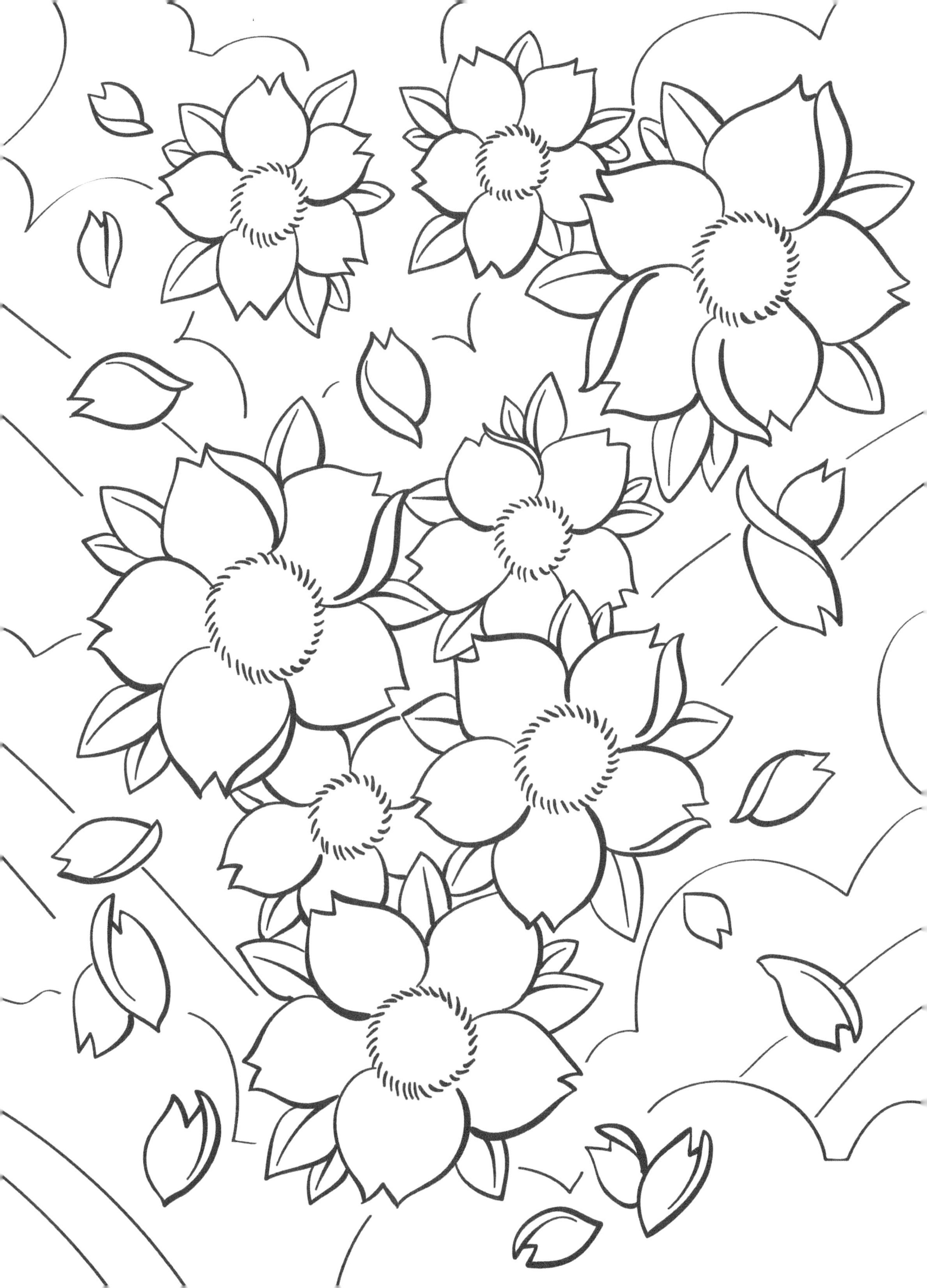

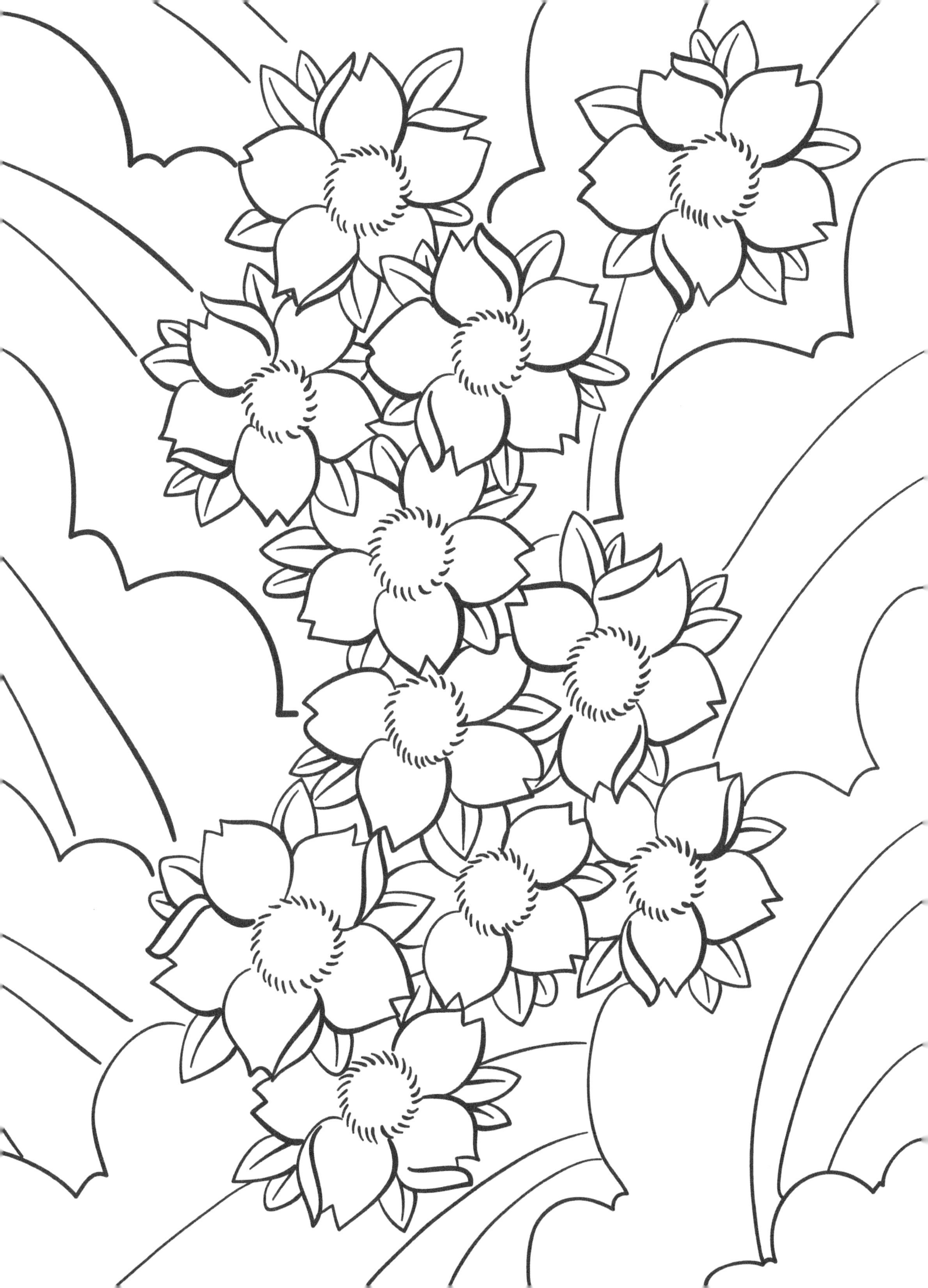

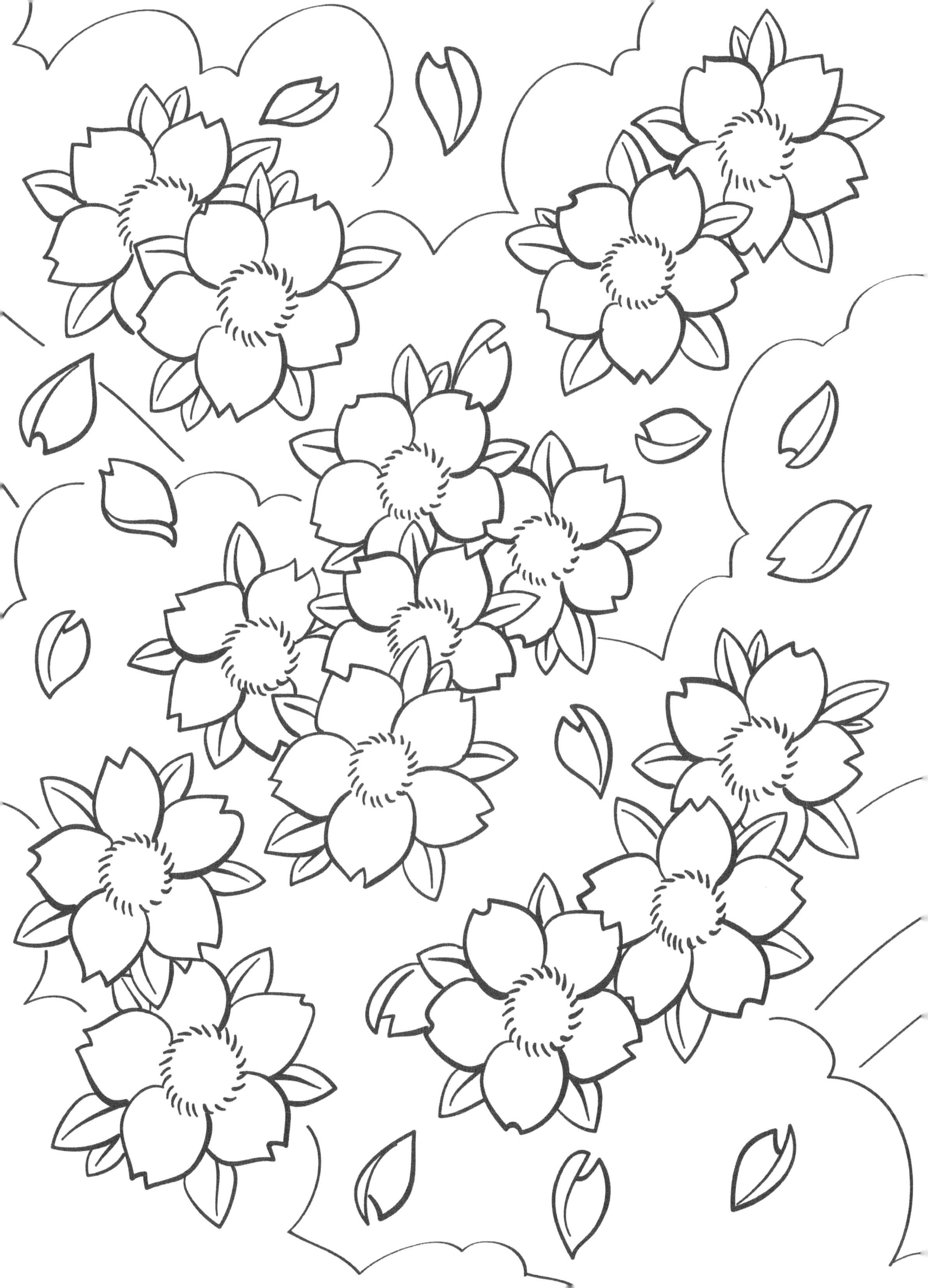

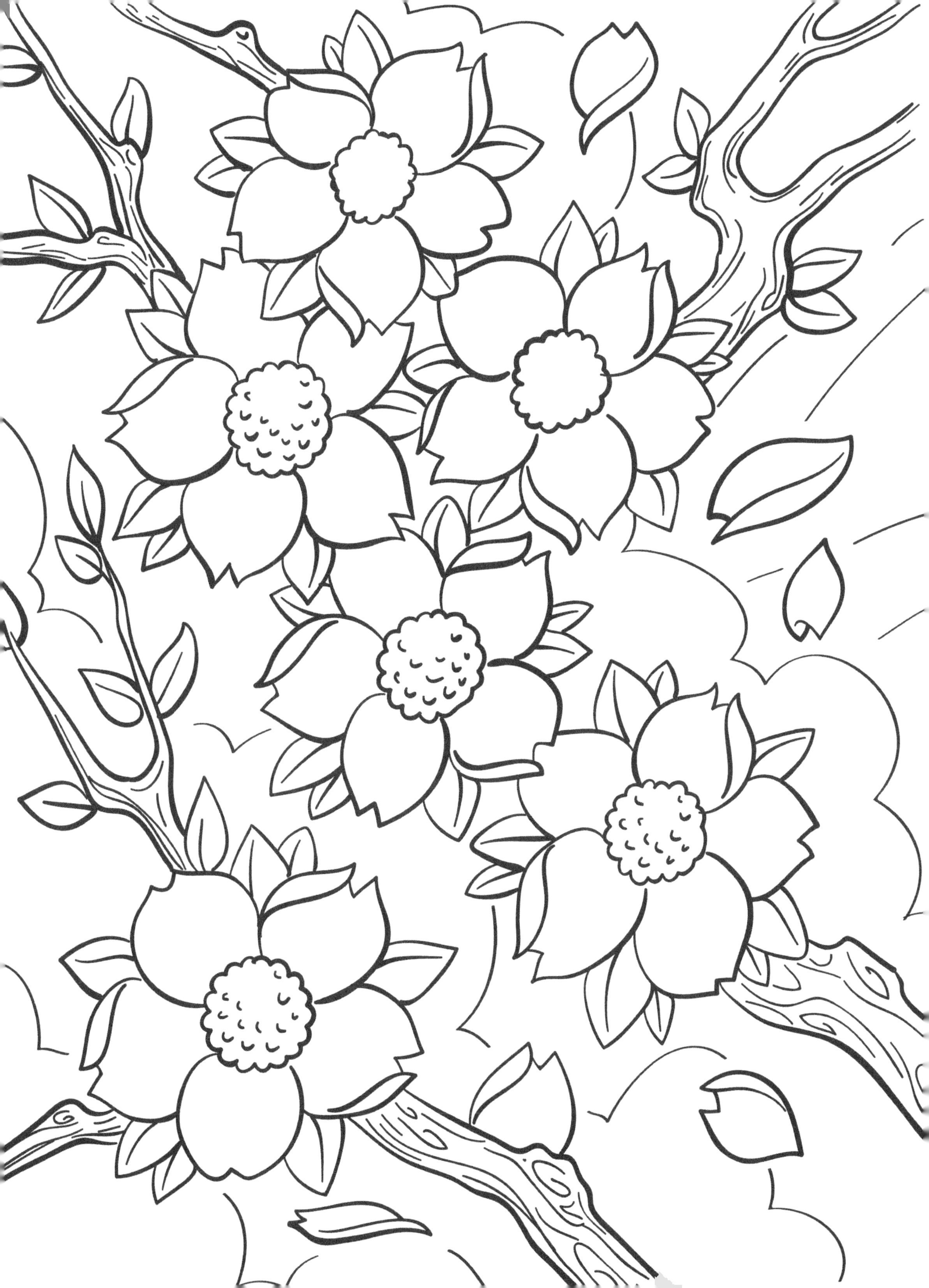

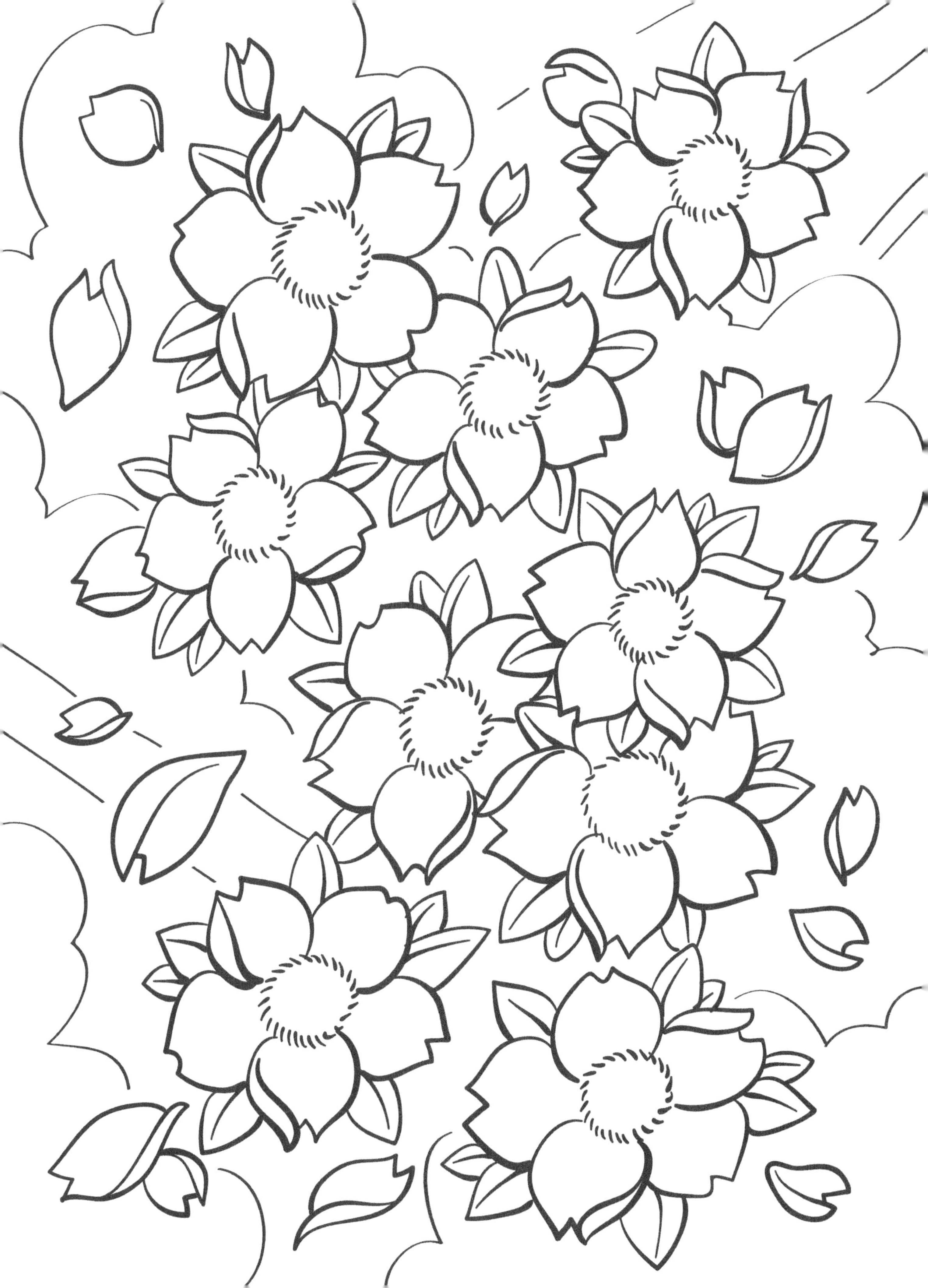

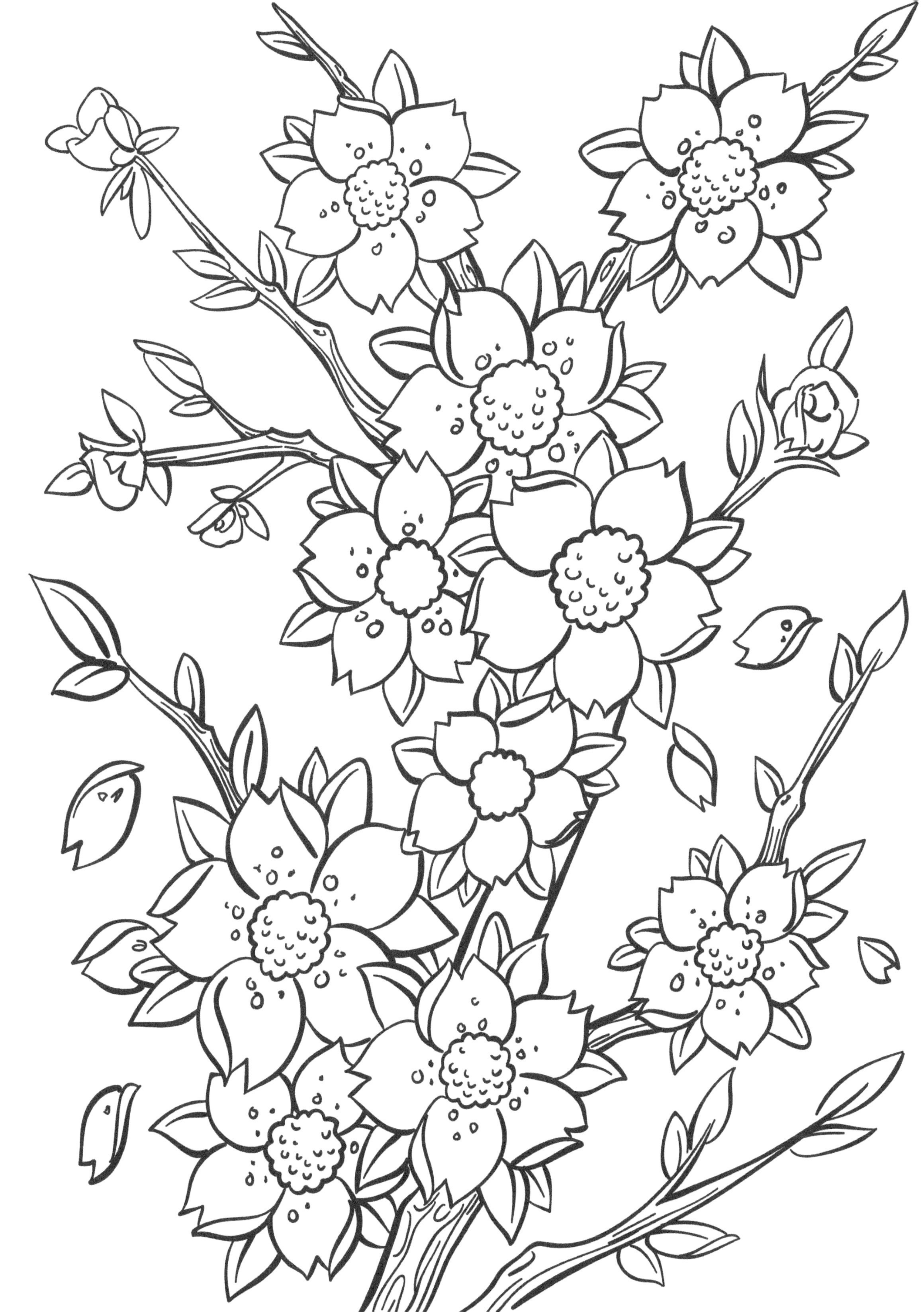

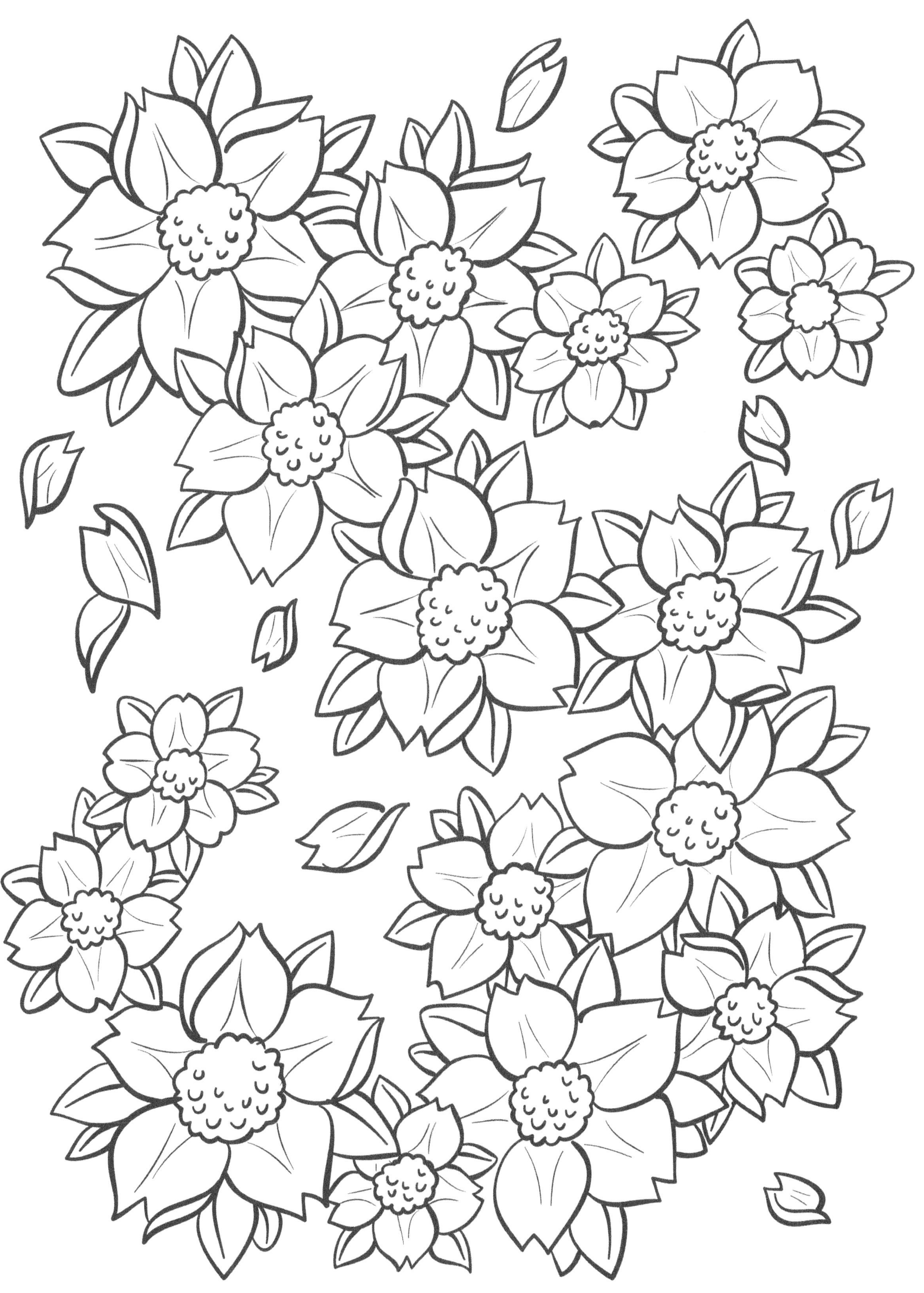

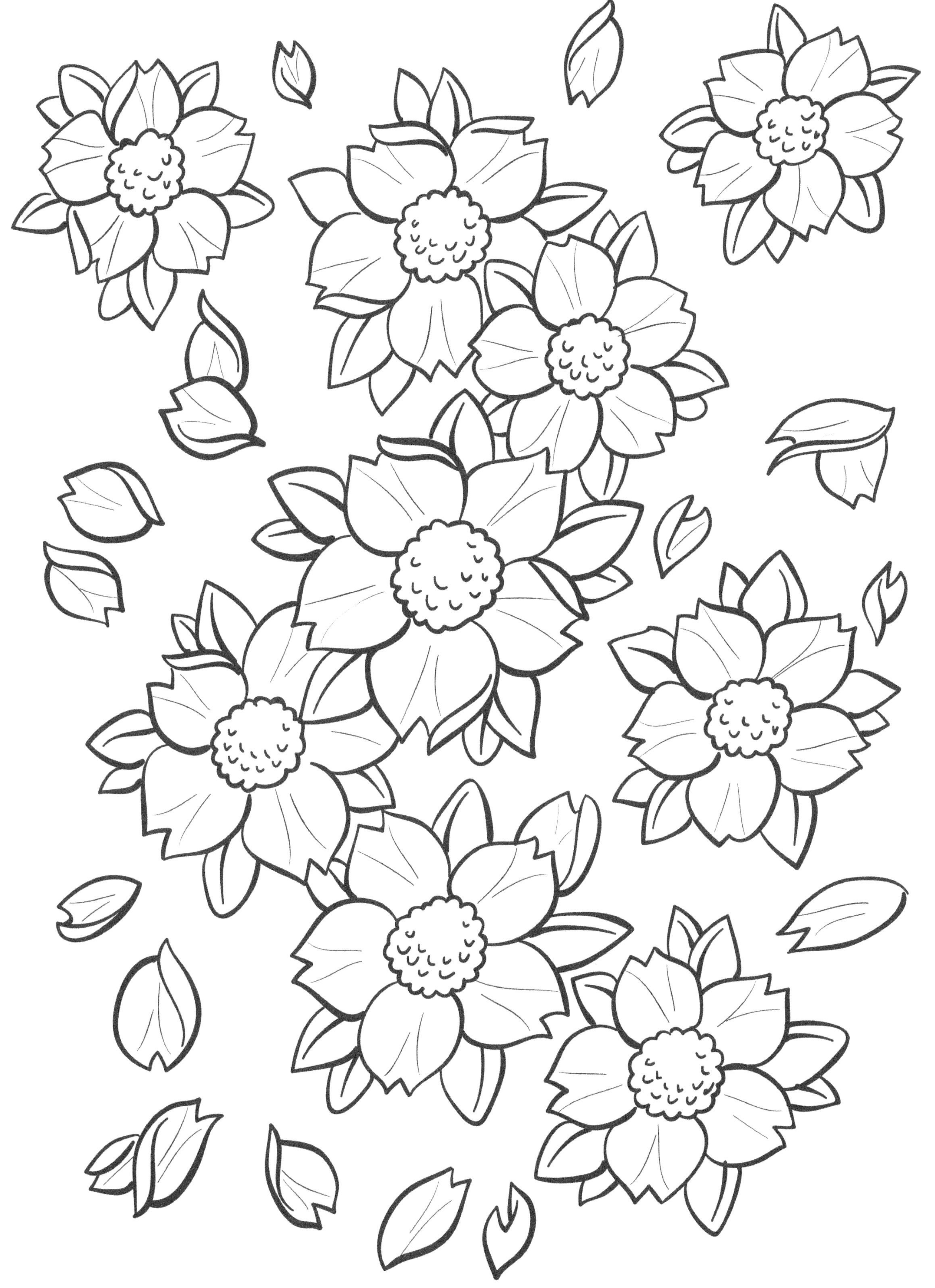

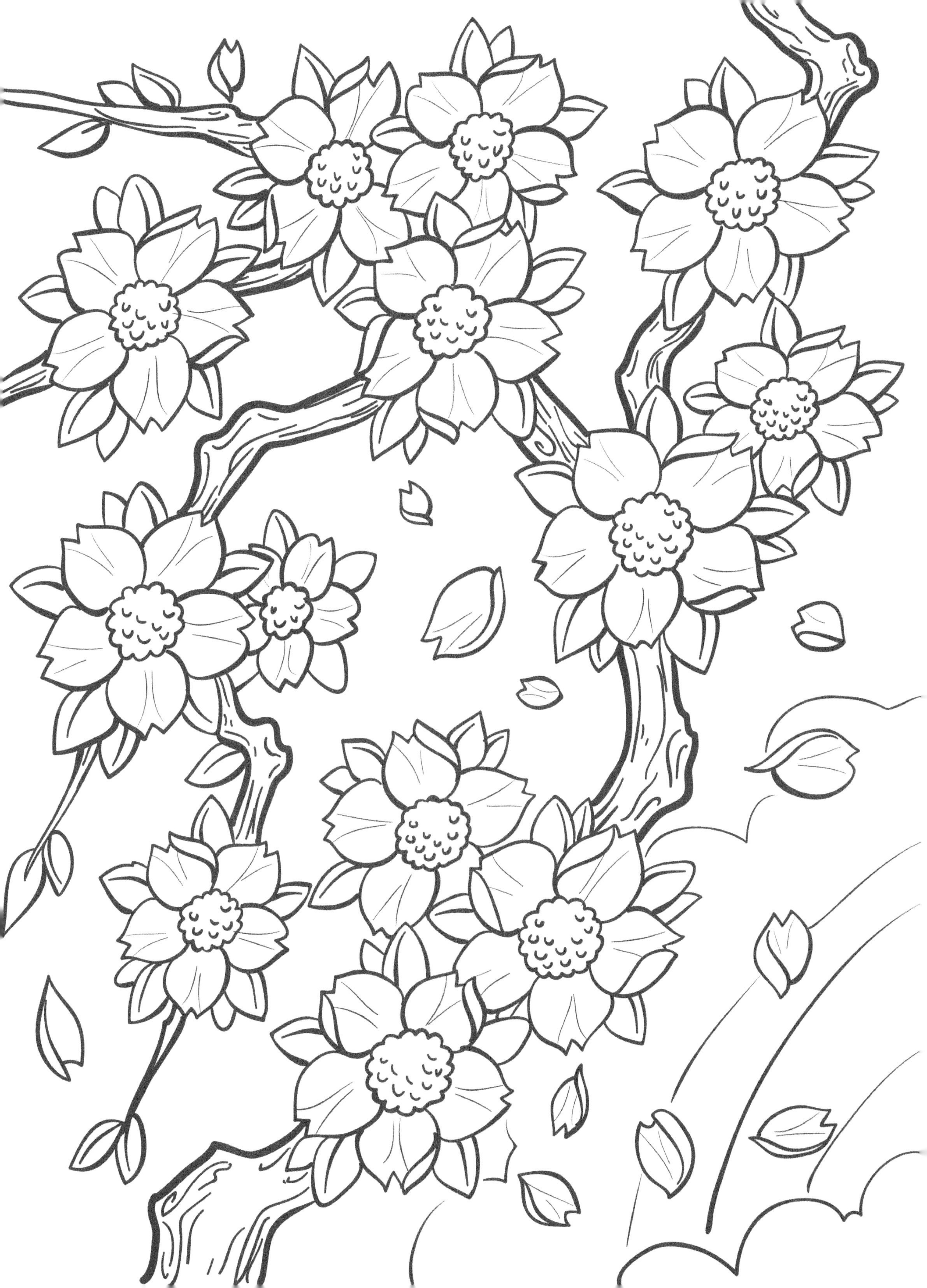

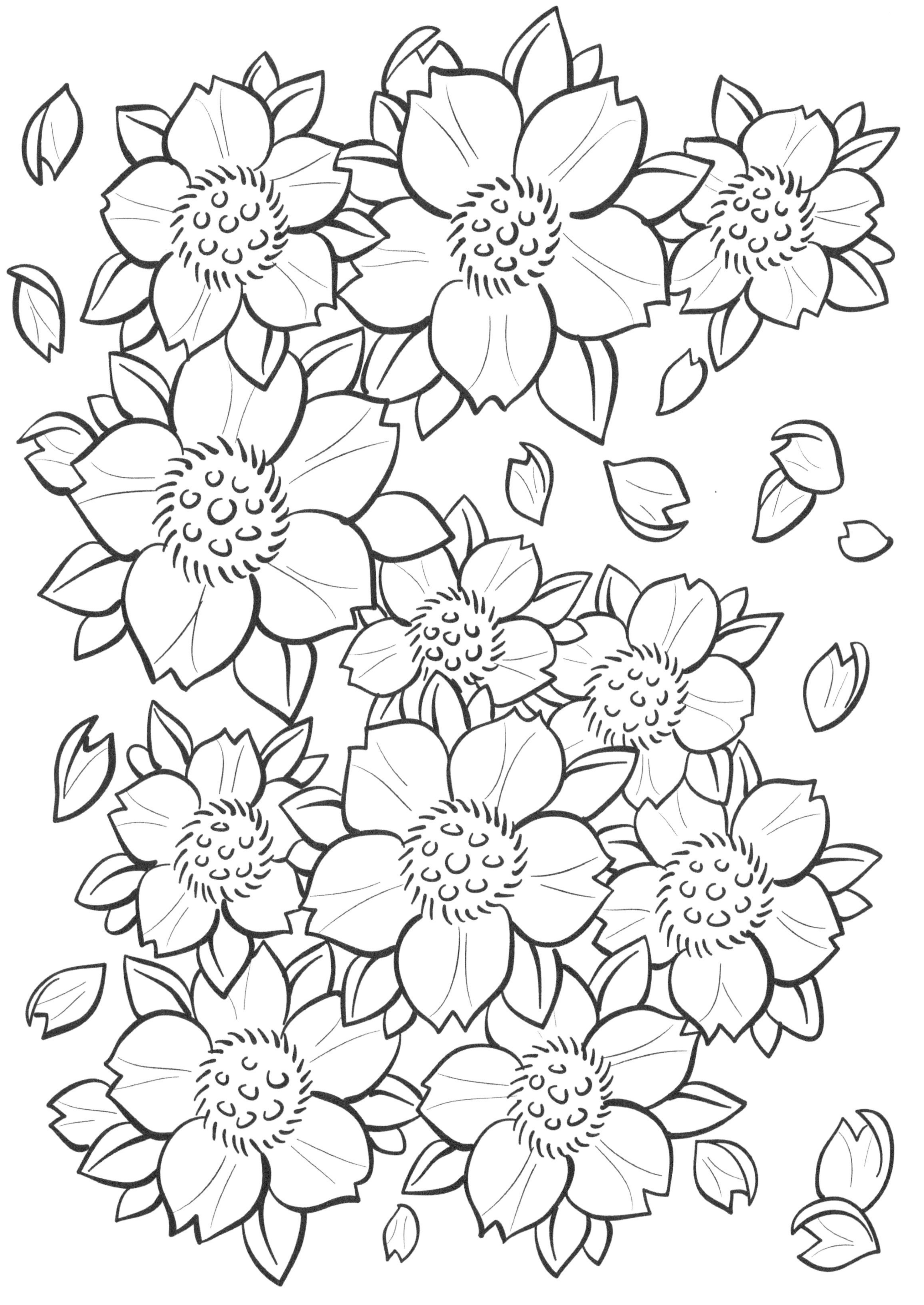

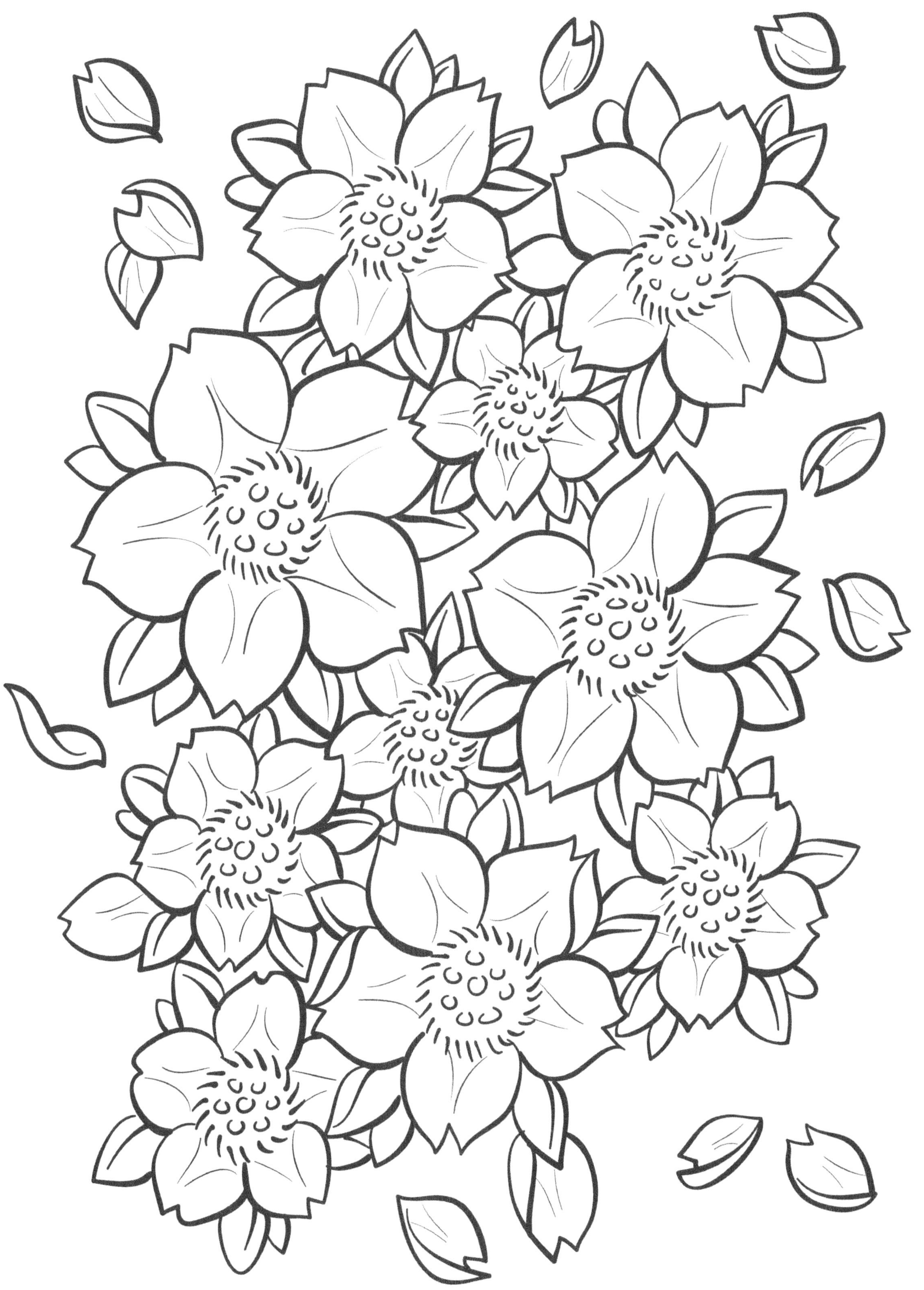

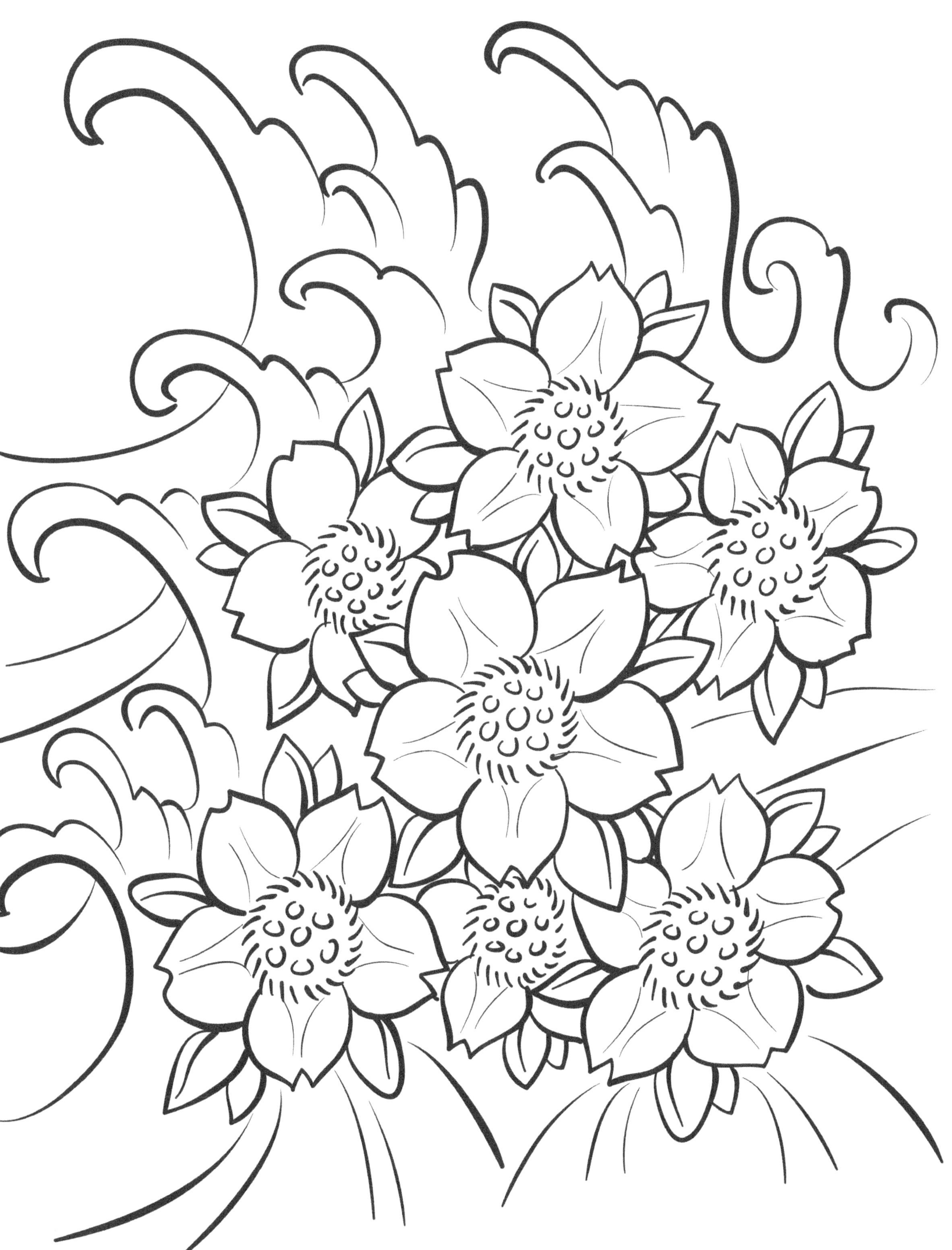

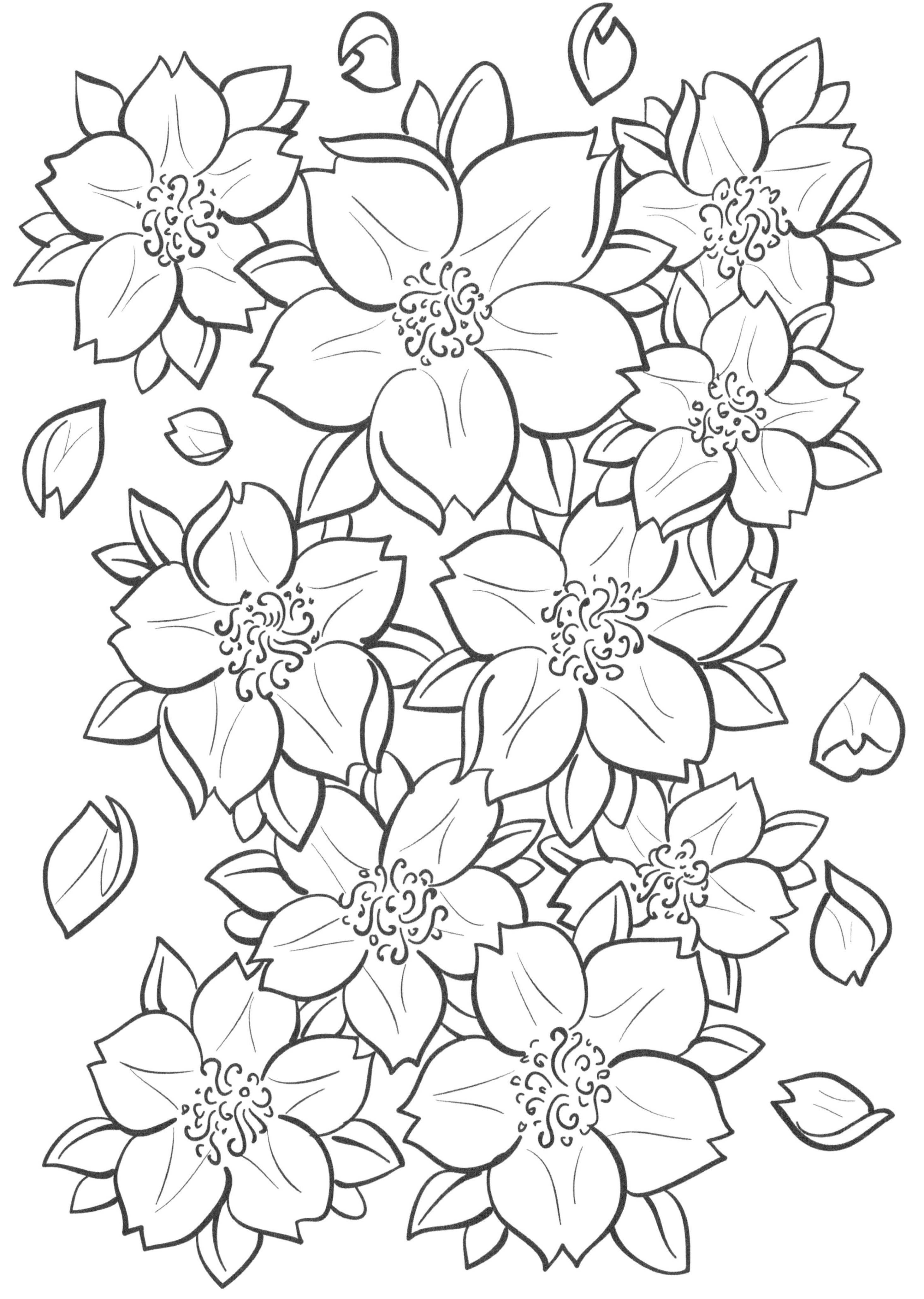

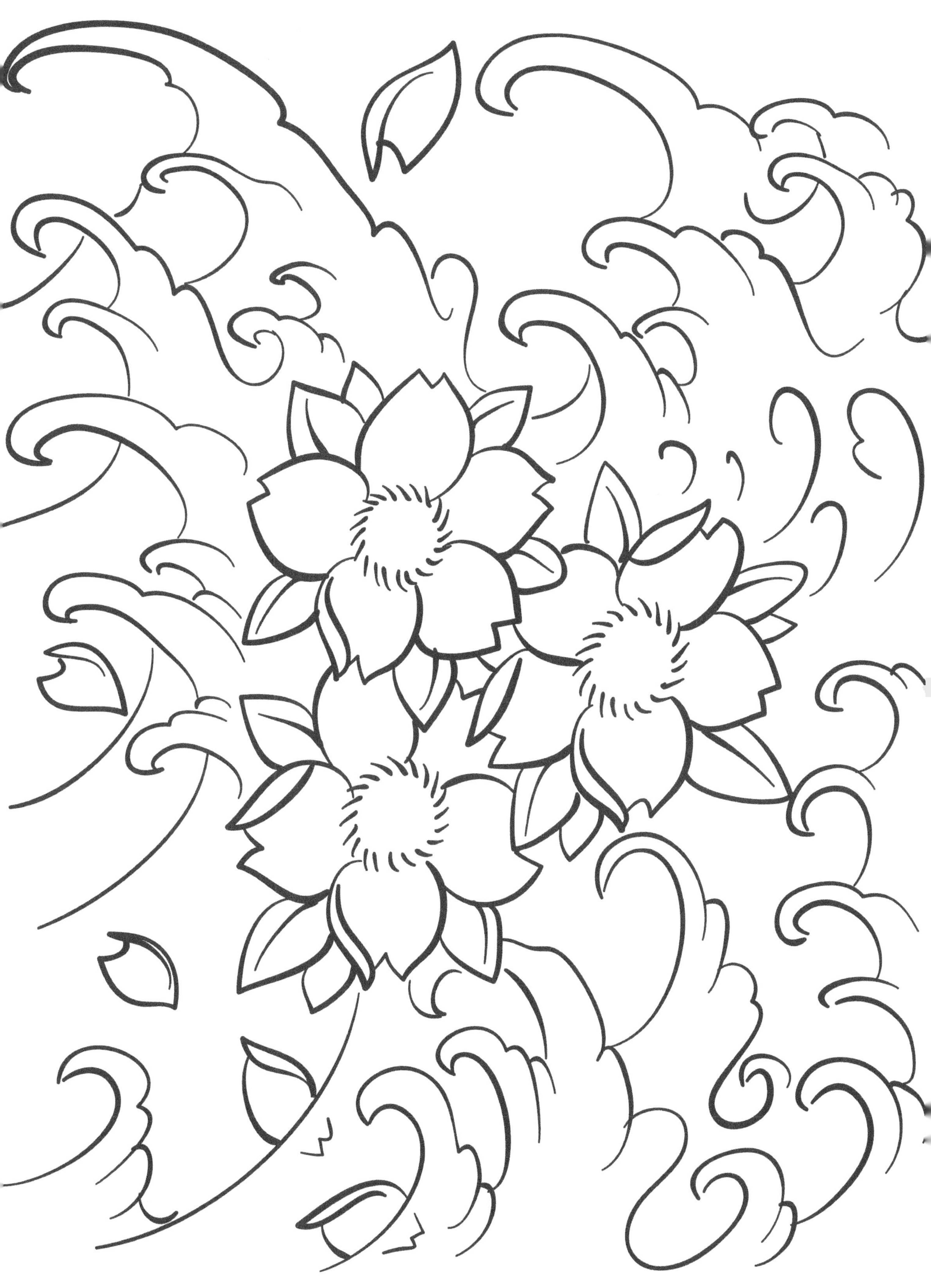

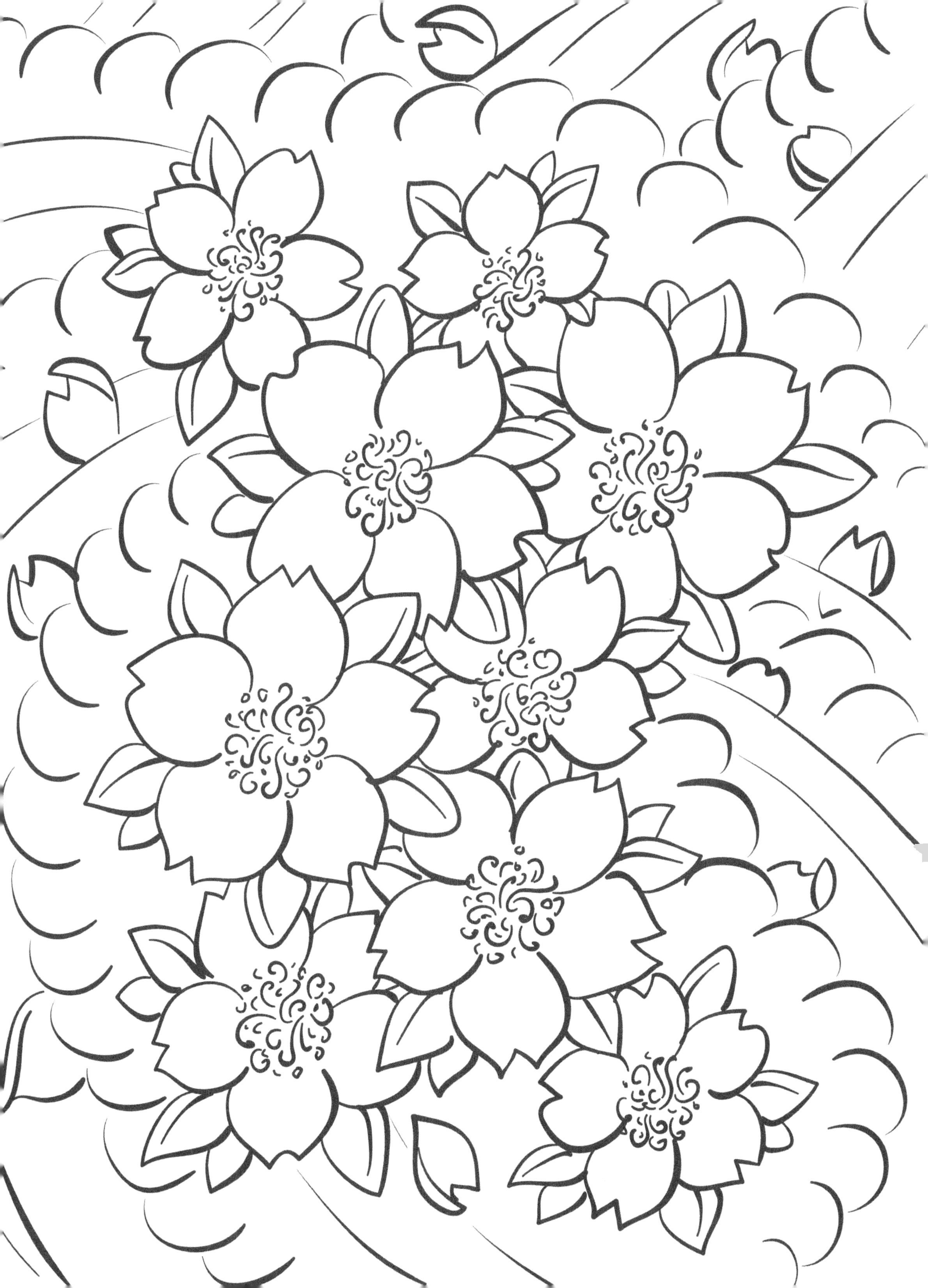

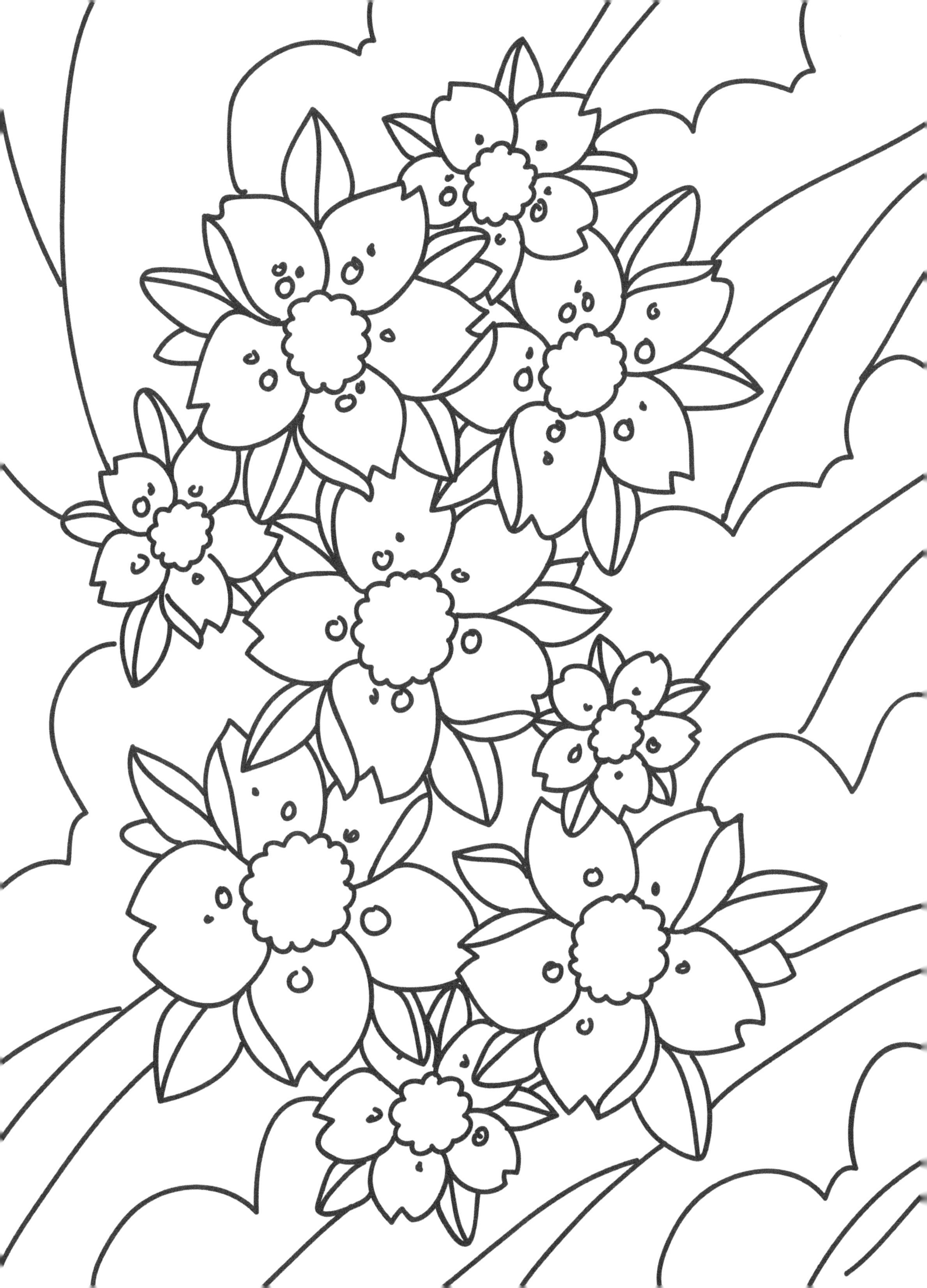

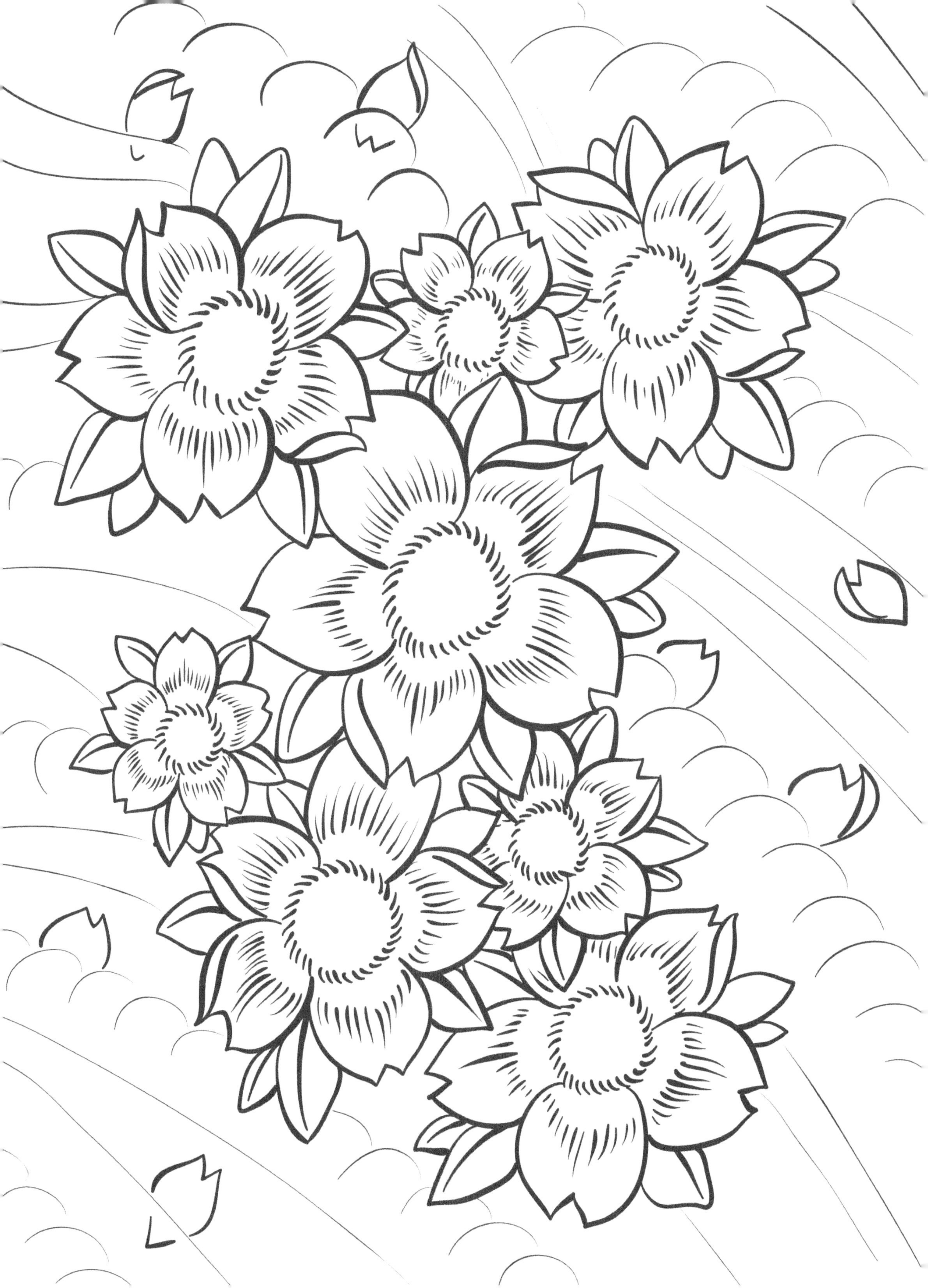

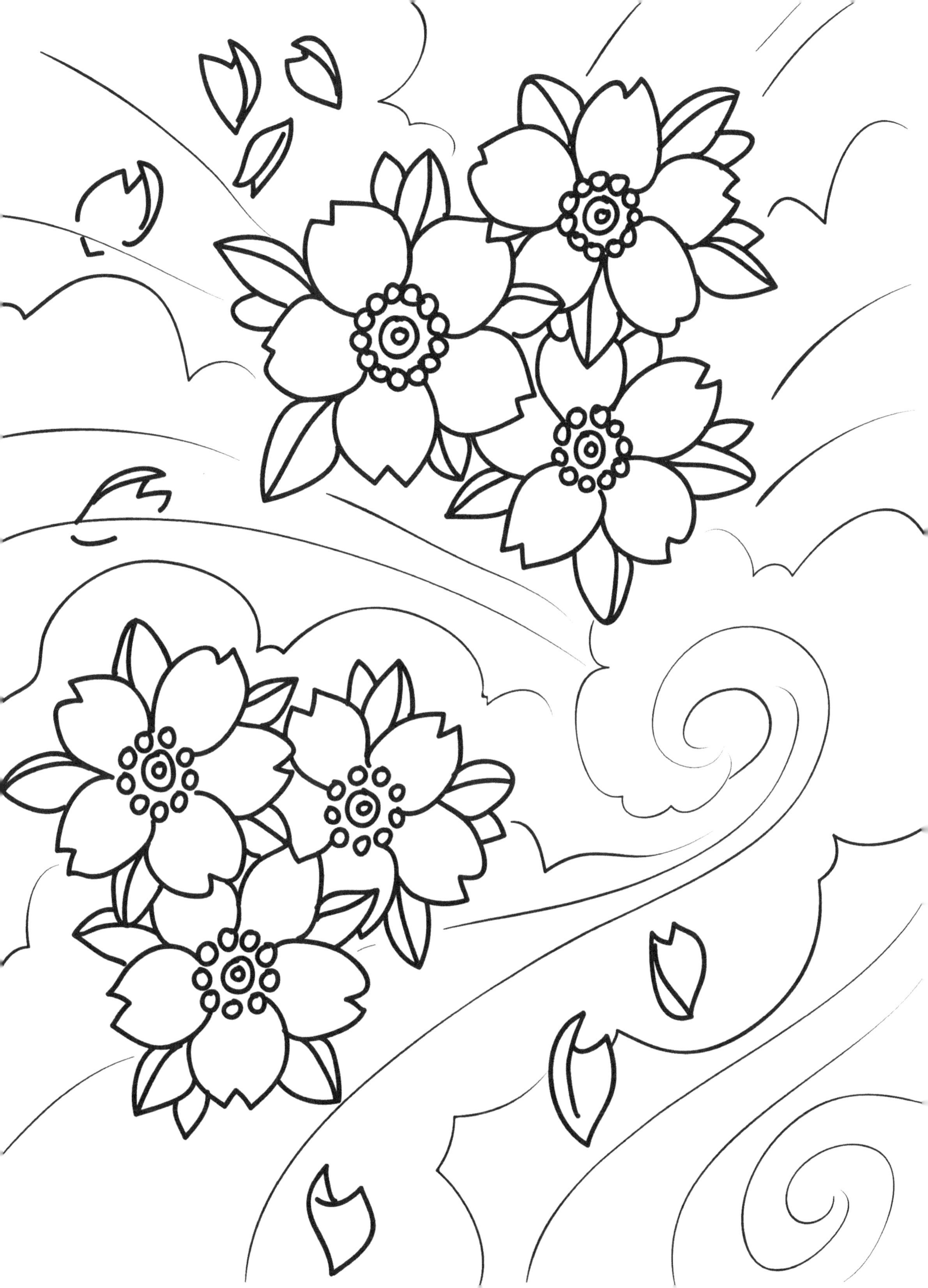

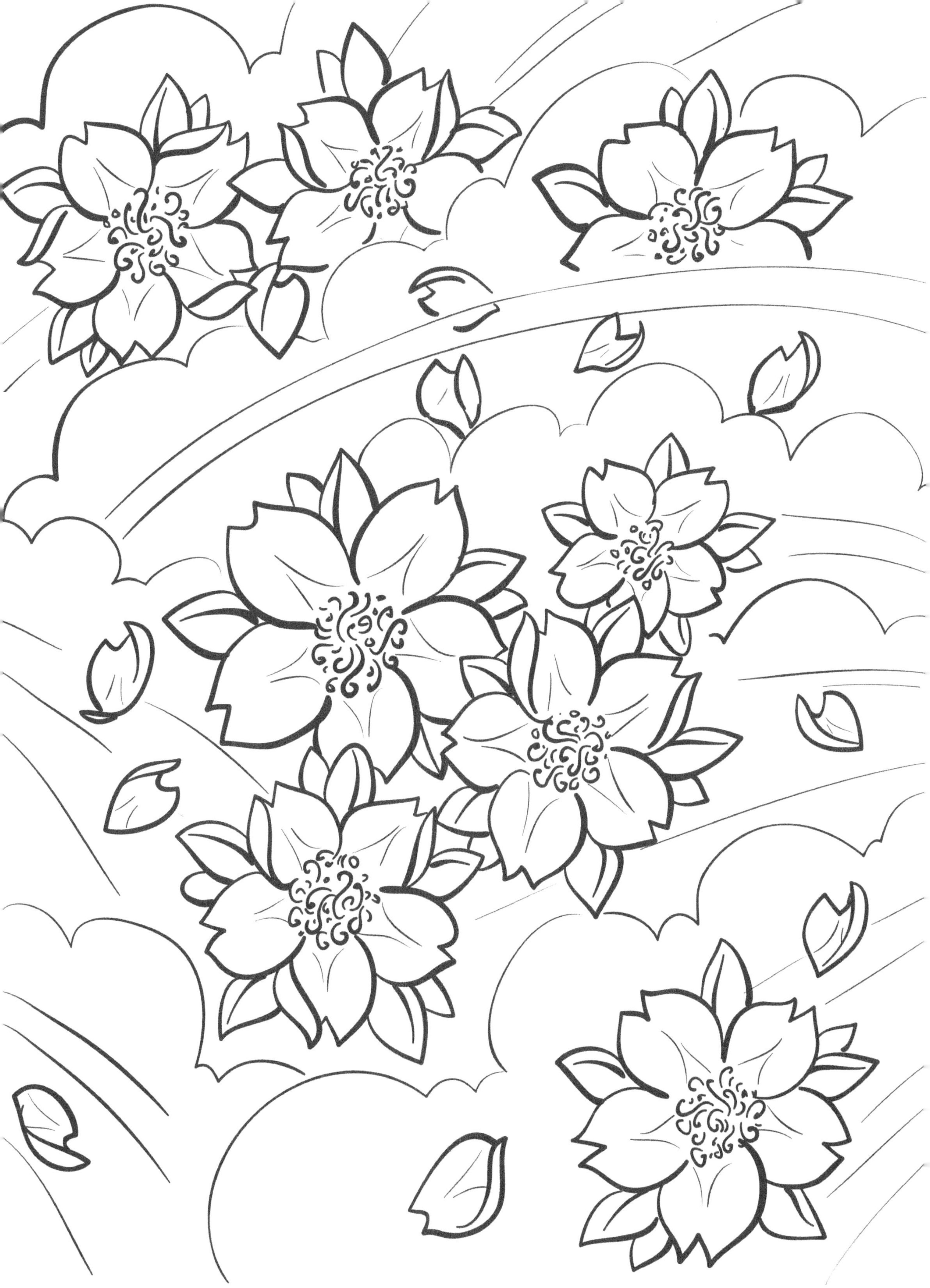

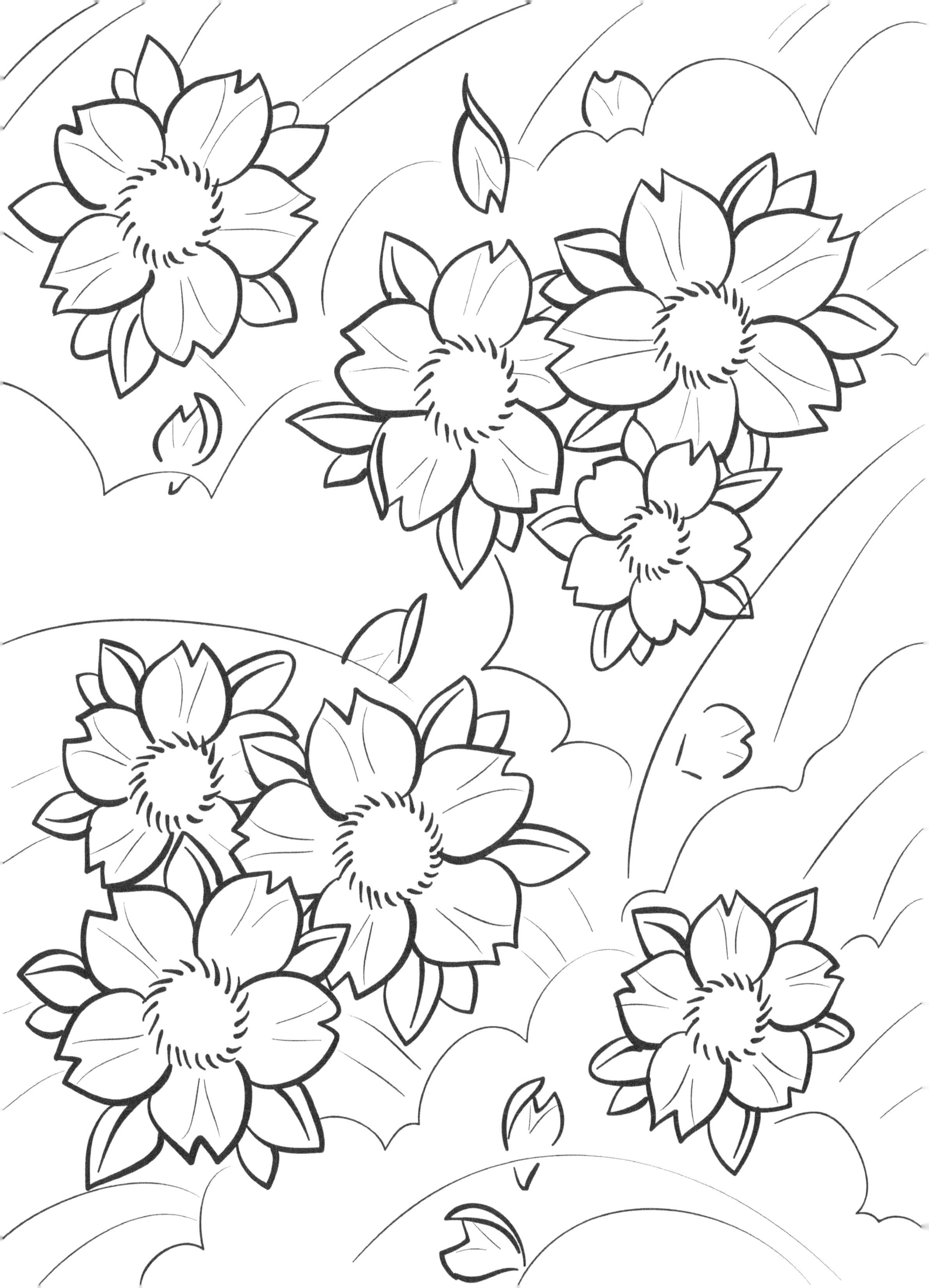

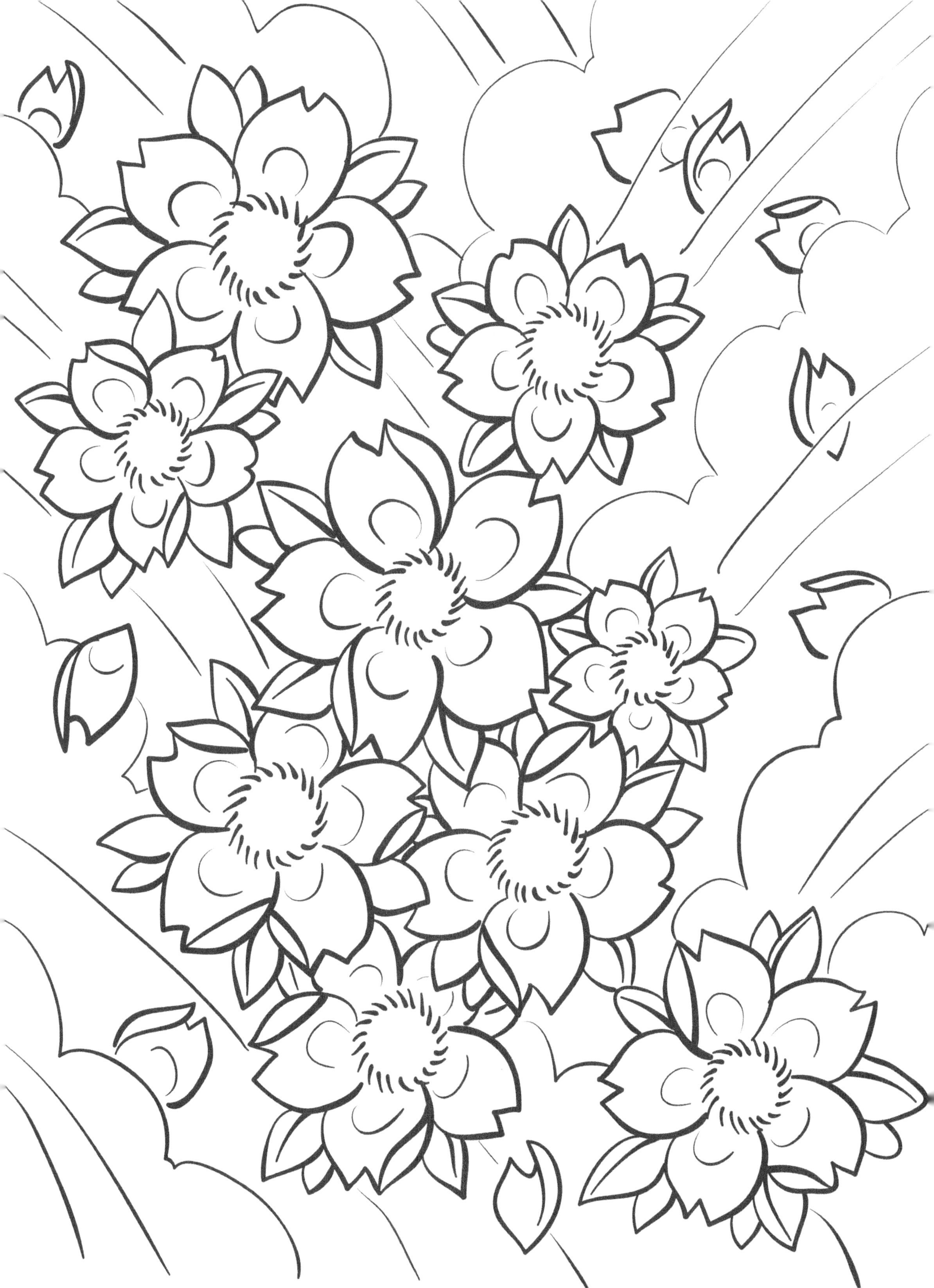

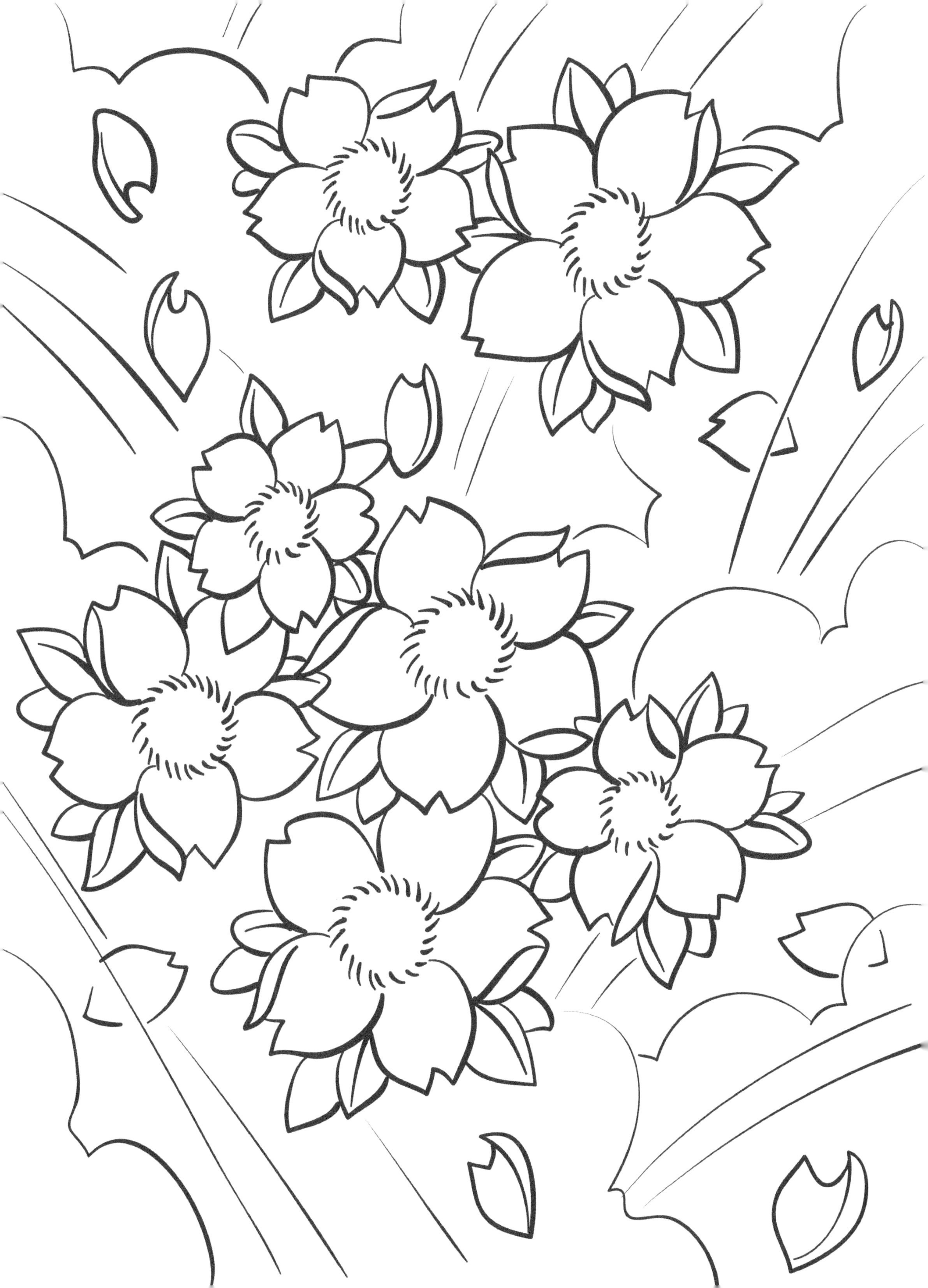

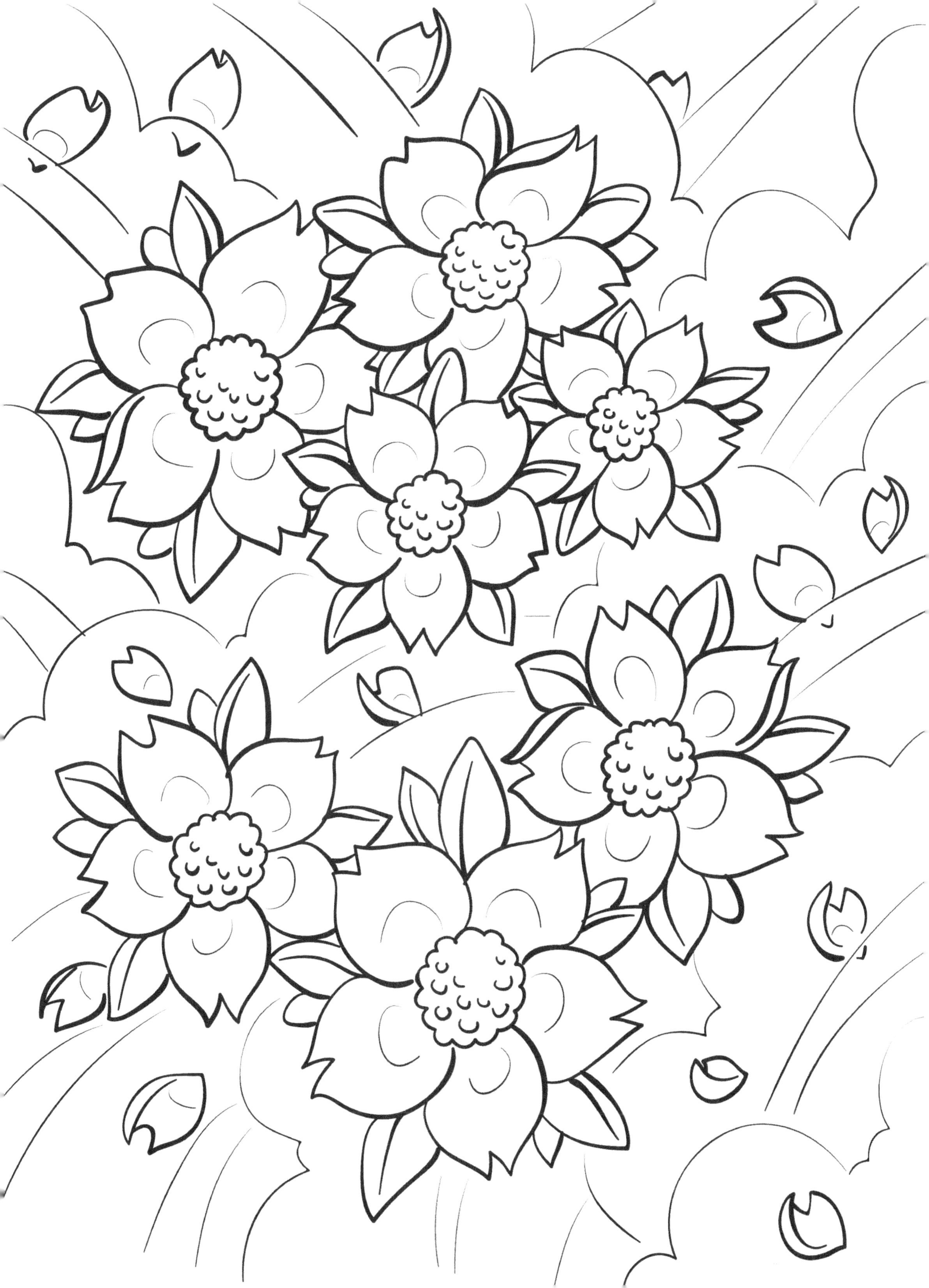

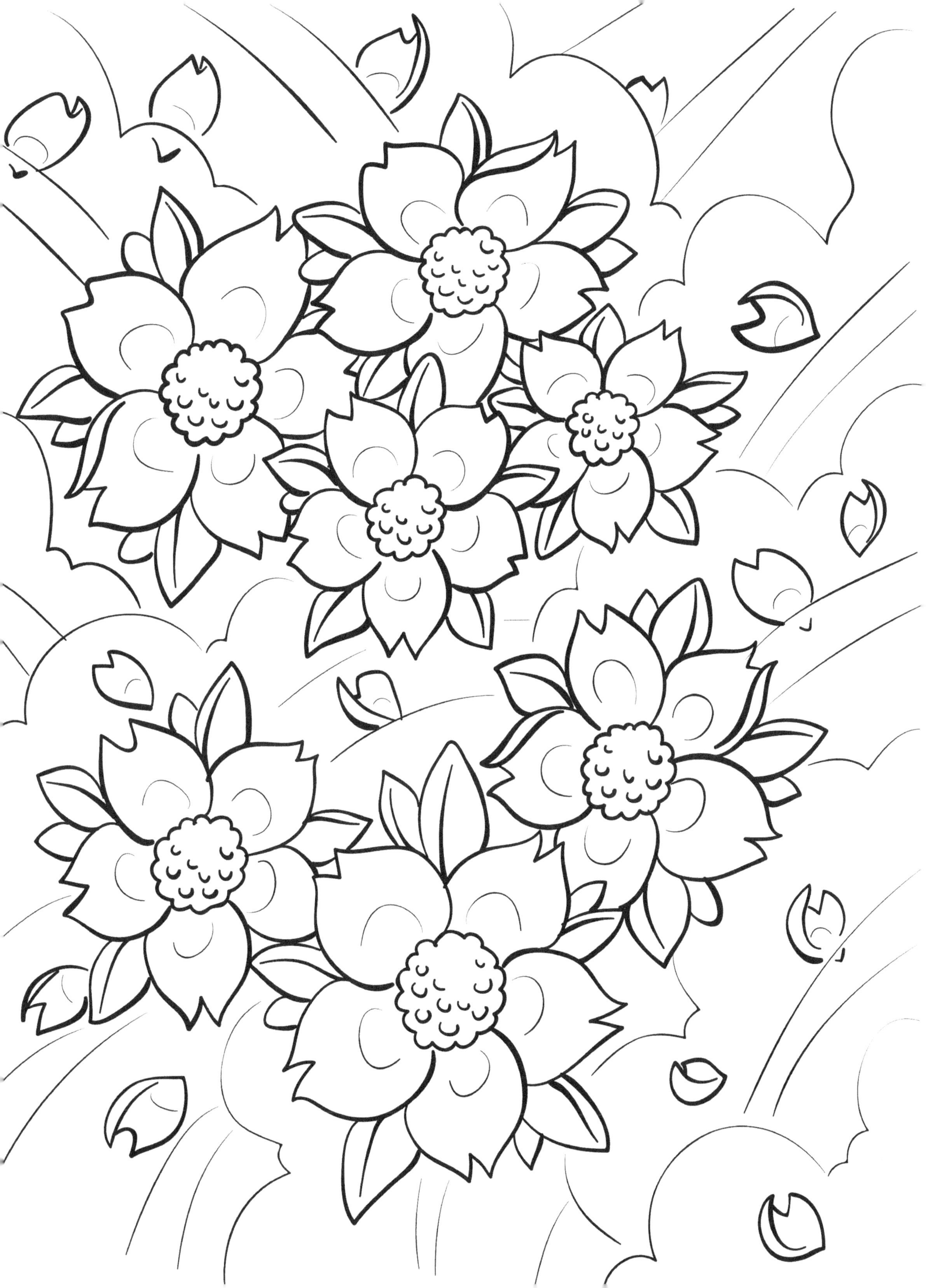

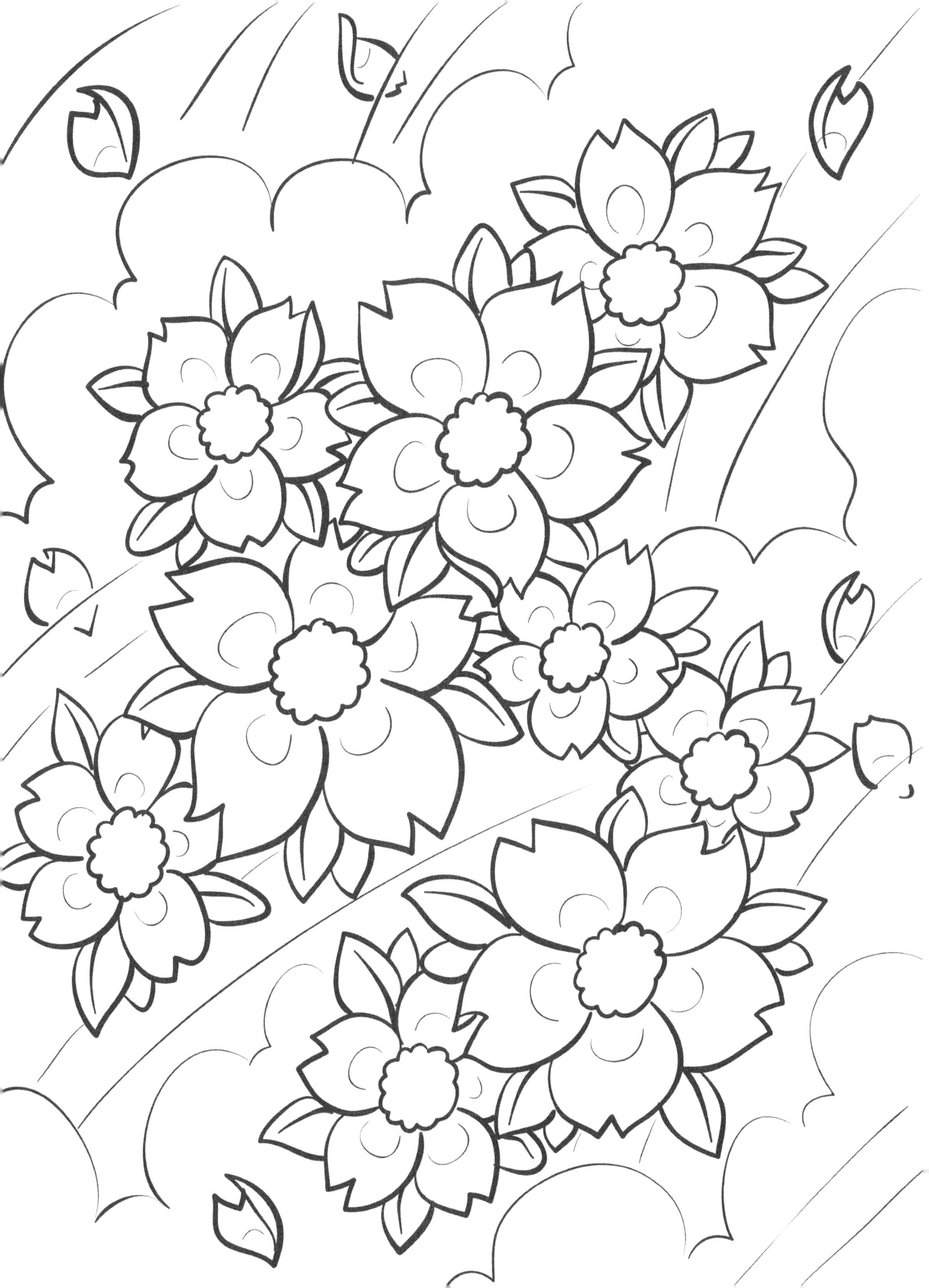

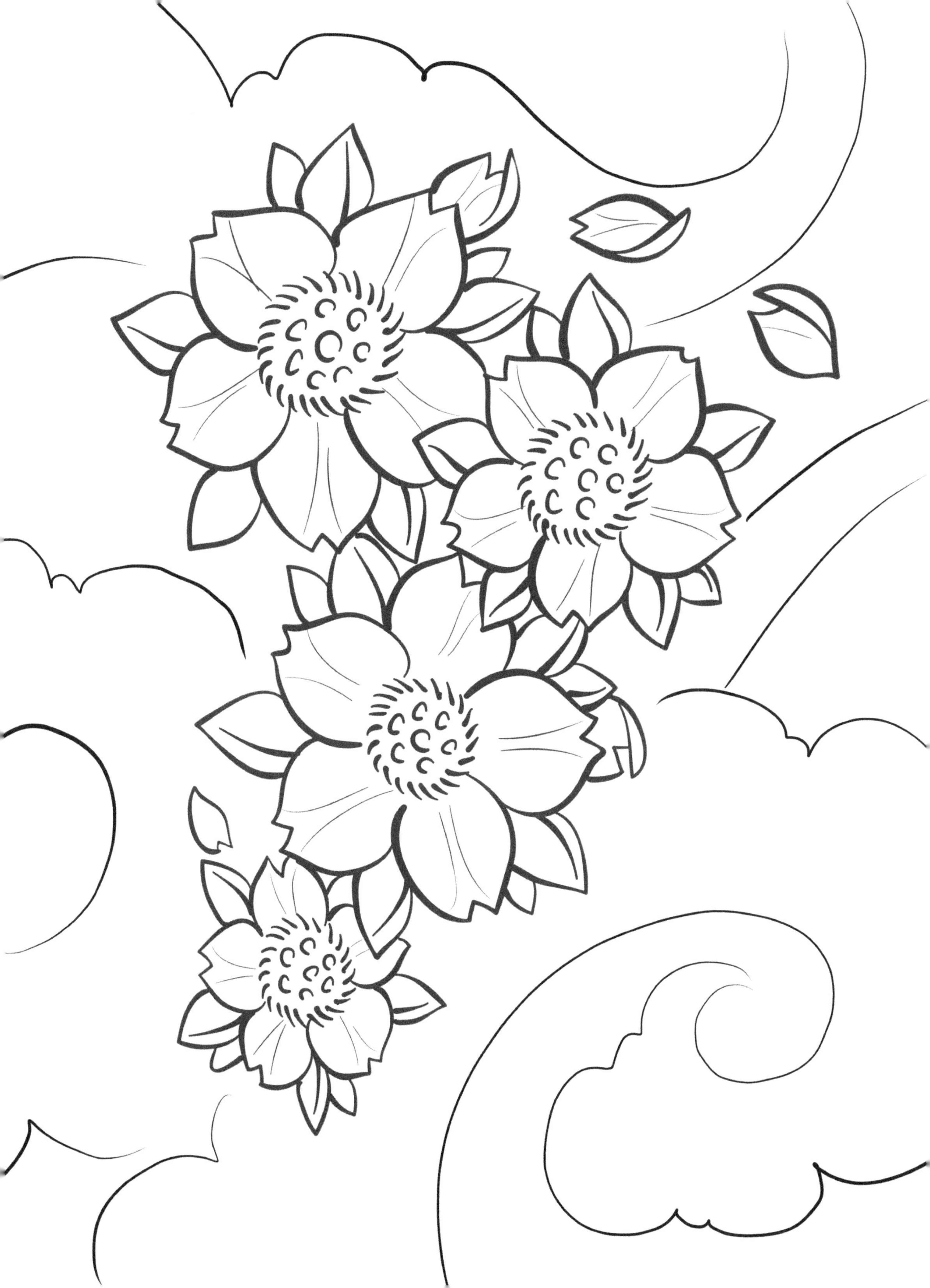